The **Cyclist's** Training Manual

A&C Black · London

Guy Andrews and Simon Doughty

The **Cyclist's** Training Manual

FITNESS AND SKILLS FOR EVERY RIDER

DISCLAIMER: Cycling in any form – from the commute to work to downhill mountain biking – can be a risky business, so always be sensible, keep alert and wear a helmet! And be sure to keep your bike well maintained and give it a once over before every ride. Finally, if you are new to exercise or you plan to significantly increase your training, a trip to the doctor for a check up is always worth while. Keep all this in mind and cycling will keep you fitter and more healthy than almost any other sport or activity there is.

Essex County Council Libraries

Published in 2007 by A&C Black Publishers Ltd
38 Soho Square, London W1D 3HB
www.acblack.com

Copyright © 2007 Guy Andrews and Simon Doughty

ISBN 978 0 7136 7741 6

A CIP record for this book is available from the British Library.

Note: While every effort has been made to ensure that the content of this book is as technically accurate and as sound as possible, neither the author nor the publisher can accept responsibility for any injury or loss sustained as a result of the use of this material.

This book is produced using paper that is made from wood grown in managed, sustainable forests. It is natural, renewable and recyclable. The logging and manufacturing processes conform to the environmental regulations of the country of origin.

Acknowledgements
All photographs © Gerard Brown
Cover and inside design by Lilla Nwenu-Msimang

Printed and bound in China.

Contents

Acknowledgements

Our sincere thanks go to...

Gerard Brown for his photography and back catalogue. Roving reporter Rebecca Charlton from www.roadcyclinguk.com. Simon's colleagues at British Cycling Coach Education Department for their input with the latest ideas from sports science. Paul West for his information on racing abroad. Tony Robinson, guru of the SRM Power Cranks. Cedric Chicken for Adidas clothing, Jim Walker for Northwave, Will Fripp for Shimano and Brian Buckle at Trek. Russell Short, Gordon Kennaway, Guy Powdrill, Tony Smedley, Nick Peacock, Paul Callinan and the riders at London Dynamo RT.

Also special thanks to Robert Foss for his patience and for pulling it all together.

Foreword

When you see the huge pack of riders in full flight coming into a stage finish of the Tour de France, see us suffer over the high mountains or empty ourselves in a time trial...

It's the training that gets us there that you don't see!

Training for five, six, seven hours a day in all weathers for years and years; the sacrifice, the dedication – this is what it takes to reach the pinnacle of the sport.

Winning Paris Roubaix in 2004 was my payback for the days as a teenager where I sat studying a huge poster of double-Roubaix-winner Gilbert Duclos Lassalle on my bedroom wall. Like all youngsters I used to say to myself, 'One day I will win that race!'

To stand on the podium lofting a huge lump of stone that you get for winning the queen of the classics was, for me, the reward for all the years that I have dedicated myself to my training.

You will achieve some success by just riding your bike, but you will miss something. Sometimes you won't be able to put your finger on what it was... Structure!

I am famous for my work ethic, but even as a professional I admit I sometimes lacked structure. I have a coach who plans my training to the letter, and I know how planning and structuring your training correctly makes a huge difference to your performance.

This book will prove invaluable to you in improving your performance and enjoyment of your cycling. It not only gives you all you need to know about skills and training – whatever your event – but it does so with a structured approach. Follow that structure and you will see the benefits.

Good Luck!

Magnus Backstedt

Introduction

Welcome to the cyclist's training manual

Cycling is a unique sport – most of us are taught the basics at an early age, often before we are introduced to any other sport. And that's it, no more help, apart from maybe a cycling proficiency test at school. Which is a shame, as anyone – no matter what their age or ability – can improve and get more enjoyment from their time on a bike, with just a little bit of effort and planning.

This book is a response to the fact that there is very little information available to help new and experienced riders improve, on both technical and fitness levels. Until now, the information that has been available has been guarded by elite coaches – which is not that helpful to anyone other than the pro riders. The *Cyclist's Training Manual* is the first resource aimed at every cyclist – no matter what their experience or aspirations – which brings together everything needed to make big improvements to both skill and fitness levels.

Who is this book for?

Quite simply, we have written this book for anyone who wants to improve in their cycling. Perhaps you're looking for a new challenge and are coming to cycling for the first time. Or maybe you want to try a new branch of cycle sport, and fancy trading in your racer for a mountain bike. Or you may have been riding in your discipline for years and are looking for some fresh ideas to help improve your results. If you are one of these people – or anyone else for that matter – then this is the book for you. All you need is an interest in cycling.

What does this book cover?

We have put the book together so that it can either be read from start to finish or you can dip in and out of chapters – depending on your experience and the advice you are looking for. The chapters progress in a logical order, but there are plenty of top tips scattered throughout that will make interesting reading if you just have a few minutes to kill before heading out on your bike.

Whichever way you use the book, we hope it helps to make you a better rider – and, at the very least, helps you to enjoy your cycling more.

- *Chapter 1: the basics* – this chapter covers everything from buying your bike and looking after it, through what to take on your rides, to finding the best places to ride and choosing the best conditions to start your riding.

- *Chapter 2: cycling skills* – this chapter looks at the skills that each cycling discipline requires. It aims to help you to find your potential best discipline by looking at the skills you have and also shows you what skills you need to develop in order to take to another discipline. It then gives you guidance and advice on how to hone these skills.

- *Chapter 3: components of fitness* – in a similar way to *Chapter 2*, this chapter looks at the specific elements of fitness that each discipline requires. It also provides an overview of fitness and training that will be essential in designing your training programmes (see *Chapter 5*).

- *Chapter 4: choosing your races* – once you have established your skill and fitness levels, the next stage is to decide whether the discipline that you are suited to is the one for you. This chapter offers an overview of each discipline, the type of riding you can do and gives you some useful guidance on how to get ahead in each – from race tactics to where to find other riders with the same interests.

- *Chapter 5: developing training plans* – this chapter takes you through a step-by-step process to develop a training programme and routine for your specific needs. It will take into account your cycling discipline, the level that you intend to ride at and all your lifestyle factors – family and work commitments, facilities and location, etc. It also contains a series of training programmes for every discipline that you can either use straight from the book, or tailor to your individual needs.

- *Chapter 6: keeping healthy* – it's no use having the skills and fitness levels to ride if you are never in shape to compete. The final chapter is all about keeping yourself healthy – from nutritional and hydration advice, to an A–Z of the most common injuries and illnesses that you are likely to experience as a cyclist. The aim of this chapter is very much prevention rather than cure!

Which bicycle sport is for you?

We cover all the main cycling disciplines in this book – what follows is a quick overview of each, and the type of events that you'll find.

Road racing

The world's finest racers take on the incredibly tough Grand Tours like the Tour de France, Giro d'Italia and Vuelta a Espana, events that bring cycle racing to a larger audience and where the participants are at the peak of physical shape. At an entry level, road racing is perhaps the hardest sport to start, which also makes it the most satisfying and rewarding. Road racing is not only about skill and fitness, it also involves tactics and – at the highest level – it requires teamwork to make the advantage. We've explained the basics here, so that you will have a better idea when you start out how to reach your goals.

Time trialling

The 'race of truth' has long been a feature of stage races and can be the deciding factor in winning overall. All the great road riders – Eddy Merckx, Jacques Anquetil, Fausto Coppi, Miguel Indurain, Bernard Hinault and Lance Armstrong – were magnificent riders against the clock. It requires meticulous preparation and specific training – all of which we cover. However it's a simple form of bicycle sport too – all you need is a bike and a stopwatch.

Track

On the face of it, track racing seems terrifying and dangerous. Nothing could be further from the truth. It is probably the safest introduction to racing for children – they have a habit of having less fear and better reactions than adults and they can learn their skills and technique on the track without the dangers of busy traffic. It gives young riders the freedom to really get stuck in. It is also a fantastic way to develop speed and technique for any cyclist and is worth a try. Don't be scared – it's great fun!

Mountain bike cross country

Mountain biking is in many ways, bizarrely, similar to track racing – it requires high levels of skill and coordination and is exhilarating, fast and furious. It's also one of the easiest disciplines of cycle sport to access, with races and training days a regular feature of all local mountain bike clubs and teams. There are fun and youth entry-level races at all mountain bike events and the emphasis is on participation and 'having a go'.

Mountain bike downhill

This is an off-shoot of cross country and developed as a direct result of wanting more thrills (and spills) while testing a rider's skill and technique against the clock. Downhill racers still need to be fit as pedalling fast and powerfully will add the essential speed and, perhaps, a podium place. No surprise then that the international downhill racers take their fitness very seriously.

Cyclo-cross

On the face of it this sport seems a little odd – riding road bikes in the mud with skinny off-road tyres and having to tackle obstacles and short run ups. It was originally invented to allow road racers to keep fit in the winter and develop technique. It is now a massive sport in it's own right in northern Europe. Like mountain biking, 'cross' – as it is also known – can be really easy to begin with as most events will allow you to use a mountain bike and all have entry level races for beginners.

Cyclo-sportive

For many cyclists the idea of racing isn't the main motivator, but a challenge is still a prerequisite for motivation. Cyclo-sportive events are timed, but usually cover long distances or courses of big races, such as the 'Etape' which is set on stage of the year's Tour de France. They are not races as such but do allow riders to test their ability and endurance. With this discipline we also include the many long distance charity rides that take place the world over.

The Basics

Introduction

This first chapter covers everything from buying your bike and looking after it, through to what to take on your rides, finding the best places to ride and choosing the best conditions to start your riding. Whether you are new to the sport or a seasoned rider, it really is worth spending some time reading these pages – these are the building blocks of all the training guidance and programmes that follow. New riders should use the headings as a checklist to make sure that you have everything covered. Experienced cyclists – we hope you will be reminded of a few golden rules that you may have forgotten along the way and perhaps also pick up some new ideas.

The bike

The first of our basics is your bike. For most cyclists this falls somewhere between a revered art icon and a well-loved companion. However, depending on how your choose it and how you set it up, your bike has the potential to be either your best friend or your nemesis.

Before you buy

There are several things that should be considered when buying a new bike. Remember, your bike needs to be an extension of your body and to fit you perfectly, so above all, you must be honest about your aspirations and your physical shape. Before you rush out and spend several thousand pounds on your new pride and joy, stop to consider the following questions.

1. Is the bike right for your type of riding – does it fulfill your aspirations and is it suitable for the kind of riding you do (or intend to do)?

2. Does the riding position suit your physical proportions?

3. Does anything hurt (yes, other than your legs from the effort!) when you ride your bike?

If you don't ask these questions – and are not truthful with yourself when answering them – you may end up buying a bike based on passion or fashion, rather than function. You may also find that you are not in the ideal physical shape to get the most out of the bike and will end up sore and uncomfortable after a few hours riding, which is likely to result in you abandoning the bike and wasting a good deal of cash.

And, despite what your long-term riding aspirations may be, don't be tempted to try to set yourself up as a pro rider. Pro bike riders are professional because they are extremely talented athletes. You have probably realised by now (or you wouldn't be reading this book) that to make it into the pro peloton you have to be able to ride a bike very fast and for a very long time. And that isn't easy (although with a bit of luck, this book will help you towards that goal).

Flexibility and the physical ability required to ride 35,000–40,000km (20,000–25,000 mi.) a year means that the bike set up a pro rider rides is never going to be suitable for the rider who rides a fraction of that distance, and can barely touch their toes. So be realistic about the bike you ride – in reality it might be slowing you down.

Lance Armstrong has a classic road style set up that allows him to pedal and breathe effectively in comfort.

Bike set up

Professional bike riders are a fastidious lot. The great Eddy Merckx was so fussy about his saddle height he often carried an Allen key when racing to adjust it 'on the fly' when descending mountains. Nothing much has changed – pro riders today are still very particular about their bike's set-up.

Despite this, there is only so much tinkering that you can do yourself. The best bet is to get advice – as with everything in this sport, this can range from the simple to the complex. At the very least an experienced rider should be able to help you set up a bike. Professional bike fitting and analysis is now very popular and readily available, so get an appointment at your local specialist cycle shop. Physiologists can also study your movement on the bike and a trained bike fitter will have experience of a variety of body types and riding aspirations, so they are well worth a visit. In other words: don't guess at it. Seek help, especially before you spend a pile of money on the wrong-sized frame or inappropriate bike.

Adaptation

It takes a few weeks to adapt to a new bike set-up. This is why experienced riders only adjust saddle height and pedal cleats by very small increments, so that their body doesn't experience any 'after shock' from big changes in set up. Try to stick with one set up as much as possible to avoid injury and to make sure your muscles are used to riding in a set position. It is not easy to copy exactly the same set up without having identical bikes but try and keep it as close as is possible.

Before you start to tweak your set up to find the perfect bike fit, get a good overall picture of your riding style. And remember that all good things come to those who wait – unless you are incredibly lucky you will not stumble across your ideal set up immediately; it will take time.

To assess your current position you can do several things yourself:

Step 1 – Video yourself during a turbo session

This will highlight any abnormalities and problems as they happen. Ask a (patient) friend to do the filming and then they can concentrate on different parts of your body for a few minutes or so.

Note: as the session increases in intensity you will revert to your worst habits. Your trunk (torso) may begin to roll from side to side, the shoulders can start to rock and you may over-reach for the pedals as your hips start to rock from side to side. It is also likely that you will shift further and further forward (or back) in the saddle.

Other things to look out for are your pedalling style and feet orientation. See how you can adapt the bike to counter these habits, perhaps by using a lower or higher saddle, or a shorter stem.

Step 2 – Look at your handlebar tape

Where is it most worn away? Where do you spend most of your riding time? Most road riders will be on the tops of the handlebars or on the lever hoods for quick access to the brakes and gears. If you find you ride most of the time with out-stretched arms with your fingers just touching the bars then it's highly likely your bike is way too long. If you spend all the time on the drops, your handlebars may be too high.

Step 3 – Take a good look at how your bike is set up

Measure and make a record of the following critical dimensions:

a) Handlebar to saddle drop – use a long level or get a broom handle (it has to be dead straight) and measure the drop from the saddle to the centre of the handlebar. Ignore the pro bike set up for a moment, this should be no greater than 10cm (4in.), preferably a lot less. For mountain biking or touring, riders usually have the saddle and handlebars close to equal heights. For cyclo-cross, the handlebars may be marginally lower than the saddle, but not by much. The longer you spend in the saddle, the less extreme you'll want the difference in height between handlebars and saddle.

b) Tip of the saddle to the centre of the handlebar – this measurement is defined by your trunk length, arm reach and arm length.

c) Tip of the saddle to the centre of each control lever (these should be the same obviously) – again this is a reach measurement, however, it can vary enormously depending on handlebar and component manufacturers.

d) The centre of saddle to the centre of the bottom bracket (your saddle height).

e) Also – crank length (see more about this in *Chapter 2*, page 36), handlebar type, width, reach and drop.

PEDALLING WITH A BELLY?

If you have a large stomach this will stop you bending and reaching lower as your legs have to travel around your rotundness on every up-stroke of the pedal revolution. Reaching lower (or further away) for the handlebars simply amplifies this. This is why much larger riders tend to ride with a very 'knees open' pedal stroke. Not only will your extra weight slow you down on the hills, it also makes for a very inefficient pe-dalling pattern. Therefore, overweight riders can be prone to knee and joint injury. A higher handlebar position may prove more comfortable but, sorry, to be more efficient you'll have to reduce the belly.

CALCULATING SADDLE HEIGHT

Here is a simple but effective method of achieving a good saddle height: have a friend hold your bike upright and sit on the saddle and place your heels on the pedals. Move the pedals so they are in line with the seat tube. Your extended leg should be straight (without stretching to reach the pedals). If it isn't, you need to adjust the saddle height accordingly. There should be no movement in your hips as you pedal backwards. Move the ball of your foot into the pedalling position and you will have a slight bend in your knee. You may have to make minor adjustments of a few millimetres up or down according to the depth of the soles on your cycling shoes, pedal type, foot size, pedalling style and event, but this is a good starting point that is unlikely to cause any damage.

Saddle height

There are many techniques for determining the correct saddle height and generally speaking you have a small 'zone' of leg extension. You are aiming to make sure your hips remain as still as possible. If your hips rock from side to side your saddle is too high. Not only will this place pressure on the back muscles as your legs stretch to reach the bottom, but also you will become very sore as you slide from one side of the saddle to the other in order to press down on the pedals.

Handlebar height

The current trend in road bikes is to have the handlebars set very low. The Aheadset has meant that the stem ends up low on the head tube and this in turn adds extra distance between the saddle and the stem. The result is usually a pain in the neck from having to crane your head or neck forward. To overcome this, many riders are rotating their handlebars or setting the brake levers further back on the hooks of the handlebars. This is not a good idea, as it makes the brakes extremely difficult to reach and operate efficiently from the drops. If necessary, reverse the handlebar stem to bring the handlebars a little higher. If you extend a line through the ends of the handlebars it should roughly bisect the middle of the seatstays.

Pedals and pedal alignment

There are dozens of different pedal systems, and all have their benefits. Clipless pedals are used by most cyclists these days, although some track sprinters still use toe straps (often combined with clipless pedals) to make sure that they stay in touch with the bike when wrenching the cranks with enormous force.

Pedal cleats need to be regularly checked for wear and for twisting – the bolts need to be tight. Worn cleats can rock from side to side and preventing the float from working effectively and may also disengage unexpectedly. Your feet need also to be

stable. Rocking feet use up energy and can play havoc with ankle, knee and hip joints.

If your feet do not naturally fall flat on the pedals, your cleats can be wedged to one side or the other and orthotic inserts made for your shoes can correct your foot plant and help your pedal stoke. This can also align the joints and miraculously solve many pedalling inefficiencies and stroke abnormalities, sometimes instantly. This is a pretty new science to cycling, but in the same way that it affects runners with their shoe choice, your foot plant also affects you as a cyclist. If you suffer from any ankle, knee, hip or back pain through riding a bike, it's well worth considering visiting a podiatrist in the first instance.

It's not just about the bike

There are a number of personal characteristics that will influence your comfort on the bike, including:

- Poor flexibility – cyclists are notoriously bad at stretching. Try to buck this trend – every minute you spend stretching will be repaid. It's by far the easiest way to avoid injury and avoid postural problems. (For more on stretching, see pages 74–77).

- Muscle weakness or imbalance – this may be either the result of injury or of another sport which creates a dominance in certain muscle groups. Either way, it is worth considering a visit to a physiotherapist or osteopath for both treatment and guidance on a suitable programme of strength training and rehabilitation to redress the balance.

- Previous injuries – again, it may be worth a trip to a medical professional.

- Sudden (catastrophic) damage – due to crashes or accidents.

- Congenital issues – how you sit on a bike can only be changed so much. It's possible that you are an 'odd' shape and this may mean you need a custom-built frame.

- Postural problems – sitting all day or standing all day will place differing strains and impact on your body. Cycling is a weight bearing activity so there isn't much strain on the body unless the position has been poorly matched somewhere.

- Leg length discrepancy – this can create a hip or back problem that is amplified by hours on the bike.

CLEAT FITTING – FORE AND AFT

Cleats in cycling shoes need to be aligned to your natural pedalling action. Go to the foot of a staircase and climb the stairs with flat feet. Hard isn't it? Now do it again using the balls of your feet on the stair treads. This is much easier, as it uses all your leg muscles to the best of their capability. For this reason, the centre of the ball of your foot should be placed directly over the centre of the pedal axle. This will mean all your leg's power can be 'expressed' into the drive train.

Ideally, your feet should be parallel with the bike's top tube, but since few of us walk with our feet like that, forcing your feet into an unnatural position is bound to create problems somewhere in the muscular-skeletal system. You need to adopt a pedalling position that is as natural as possible. Most riders usually have their heels slightly inboard of their toes. But don't worry if you find that your preference is different to your riding companions, or even if you have one foot different to the other. The important factor is to pedal comfortably without stress or injury.

Mountain bikers use their body to stay loose across technical trails, as they ride 'compact' with bent arms and legs – this needs to be considered in the fitting process.

Fit specifics

Many of the points covered above are generic to cycling and do not take specific disciplines into consideration. Here are a few more things to think about in the pursuit of the perfect riding position.

Mountain bike

If you are serious about riding off road, you must ride your mountain bike as much as possible. Add some slick tyres for winter road training to get used to your racing position. Many seasoned pro mountain bike riders own just one mountain bike and this allows them to have a familiar riding position all year round. If, like many pro mountain bikers, you swap over to a road bike for part of your training or racing, keep your two positions as close to one another as possible – even if this means a marginally less aerodynamic road position.

Unlike road bikes, aerodynamics are not as important on a mountain bike – comfort and control are the key elements. The front ends of many mountain bikes are usually quite high, which makes it much easier to set the handlebars in the appropriate 'sit up and beg' position, with the saddle set at a similar height. When once long stems were favoured on mountain bikes, today's preference is for shorter bikes with compact frames, for greater agility and control.

Cyclo-cross

Most cross riders adopt a similar position to their road bikes but with the handlebars slightly higher and closer. This position provides better control at slow speeds and faster steering, as well as making the bike more manageable on steep descents. Saddle height may be fractionally less than for road riding partly to lower the centre of gravity, but more significantly to make leaping on and off the bike a little easier (especially with a cross bike's higher bottom bracket).

Cyclo-cross riders have to work hard on their technique and therefore the bike set up will be tweaked to gain the best combination of slow speed handling and comfort before flat out aerodynamic road speed.

Time trial

A time trial requires a powerful and consistent effort but it is also where position can play the biggest part in performance. If you watch riders in a time trial or study pictures of them, you'll notice how much their positions vary from one rider to the next. This is an area where amateur riders make the most mistakes. For example, if you can ride at 50kph (30mph) for over an hour you may want to consider a more aerodynamic position than a rider who rides at less than 40kmph (25mph) over a similar distance. Remember, comfort will determine how far and how fast you can travel – aerodynamics is just the icing on the cake.

Cyclo-cross also requires a compact position for riding technical courses – a higher bar and break/gear lever position will help with jumps and obstacles.

If you have two bikes, copy the set up of your racing bike onto your training bike and train in the position you are going to be racing in. Specialist time trial riders in the propeloton ride at least once a week on their TT bikes, even during the winter, so that they can constantly remain familiar with their more extreme aerodynamic position. Some even use their TT bike for specific speed work and have it set up on a turbo trainer so they can do intervals in their TT position.

Opinions on aerodynamics in cycling are very involved. However, everyone agrees that the best way to go faster is to use the most aerodynamic, yet still comfortable, position you can. This should come before you start to worry about disc wheels, aero helmets and expensive machinery. In fact, there is plenty of evidence to suggest that a properly set up TT bike with standard wheels and equipment is far faster than a badly set up aero TT bike with the latest kit on it.

Aerodynamics is not as simple as merely getting the front end as low as you can manage. Chris Boardman's TT bike was set at such an extreme position that riders of a similar stature would struggle to ride it for 10 minutes. But as he has pointed out, his body shape allows him to sit happily in an aero tuck whilst riding to the shops. But not everyone is so lucky. Compare his position to that of Miguel Indurain or Lance Armstrong – these two superb TT riders were unable to achieve the same low aerodynamic position, but they rode just as fast because they could harness their power through positions that were comfortable and efficient for them.

This is a very aerodynamic position, yet it is not too stretched out or restrictive to the time triallist's pedalling efficiency.

Triathlon or aero handlebars

These handlebars first came about in the RAAM (Race Across America) in the mid-1980s and were actually first designed for comfort as they allowed the riders to rest their arms on the arm pads and still steer the bike. But the result achieved not only comfort but was also very aerodynamic allowing the rider to assume a downhill skiing type tuck, with the arms providing a penetrating element for a much more aerodynamic shape. This was adopted to great affect by triathletes who copied the RAAM position. The handlebars eventually reached mainstream cycling when Greg Lemond first used them to win the Tour de France in 1989 in dramatic style in a 25km (15mi.) time trial on the final day, beating Laurent Fignon (who rode a standard TT bike of the day) by 58 seconds gave him the overall victory by just 8 seconds – the closest ever winning margin.

To a large degree, the shapes and dimensions of your handlebars and aerobars determine how low you can get over the bike. However, if your reach is too long this can affect the steering and if you opt to place the gear controls at the ends of the handlebar extensions you may find that they are a bit of a stretch. Your flexibility, along with your arm and torso length will play just as big a part as your height and leg length to achieve your optimal position. If you set your handlebar height too low, you may well experience neck and back pain, especially in the longer events. It's worth considering a higher handlebar position (or even using a road bike set up) if you are going to ride for longer than 80km (50mi.). When you first experiment with aerobars, use a set that allows for a lot of adjustment so you can experiment and adapt your position.

TT SADDLE HEIGHT

The popular opinion has been that a TT bike should have a higher saddle position than a road set up, but recent research states exactly the opposite. The lower the position at the front, lower the the saddle height needs to be dropped. Why? Well, by leaning further over and subsequently further forward of your usual road position you are tilting your hips forward further, which effectively lengthens the pedalling stroke and therefore raises your saddle height for you. A reduction of up to 2cm (1in.) is sometimes needed to retain the same power output when in the TT tuck.

The standard endurance track position is on the drops of the bars and with a lower saddle position to allow the hips to rotate forward and maintain power.

Track

On the track, power is the key element, even over comfort. However many endurance track riders (who are usually road riders as well) adopt the same position on all of their bikes. The common mistake is to raise the saddle height in the quest for more power, when lowering the saddle is actually the true way towards a more powerful position, as it allows you to recruit more muscle power into the pedal stroke.

For sprinters, handlebar height and reach is usually lower for better aerodynamics and to make it easier to pull up on the handlebars and bring more muscles (in the back and arms) into use. However, you are less likely to use the upper part of the handlebars (unless riding the Madison) so this should be considered when settling on a position. Sprinters can travel at 60kph (40mph) or more, so control is also vital – don't be tempted just to fit a negative rise stem and the deepest set of drops you can find – experiment with your sprinting position. Whereas in the past sprinters always preferred a very low handlebar height with narrow bars, the current trend among top sprinters is to raise the handlebars for more open arms so they can fill their lungs more easily and bend their arms more to reach the lower sprinting position. If the handlebars are set too long and low, your arms will be too straight. This is no good for match sprinting where the riders throw the bike all over the place.

LOOKING AFTER YOUR BIKE

1. Change your tyres regularly	Tyre choice is down to experience and personal preference, but changing your tyres long before they wear out is key to speed and safety. As tyres wear thinner they will be more likely to puncture and grip will begin to get more unpredictable. This can be lethal, so keep a stock of tyres and swap the back for the front from time to time to keep the wear consistent (the rear tyre wears out quicker).
2. Watch out for road debris	Prevention is better than cure, especially when it's wet and cold. If you ride in all weathers you will get more punctures. If you ride in the gutter and through parks and subways you are more likely to flat. In rain debris is washed all over the road and you are more likely to catch a flint or shard of glass.
3. Learn how to fix a flat	Fixing punctures is an essential cycling prerequisite. Practice is essential for speed, but anyone can fix a flat if they have the time and patience. Ask a shop mechanic to show you if you are not sure (they have to do this ten times a day, so they are usually quite good at it!) and in time you will get quicker.

4. Pre-ride check

Look over the bike. Does anything look unusual? Are the cables frayed or does the outer cable look kinked or broken? Has the chain gone a little slack? Do the brakes have any pad wear and do the brake levers work smoothly? Pick up the bike and (gently) drop it, does anything rattle? Check the tyres, especially the treads for flints and wear.

5. Wash your bike

Having a clean bike is the first step to having a well running bike. You get close to the workings and are more likely to spot the signs of wear and tear. Wash your bike as soon as you return after every rainy or muddy training session. Dry it off and lube the chain, so the bike is ready to go next time.

6. Have a regular service

If you are busy and never have the time to prepare your bike properly then find a local bike shop and build a good relationship with them. Good bike shops usually have good customers and they will have busy work-shops. Bike mechanics are a loyal bunch who take pride in what they do, so treat them well. Then if your bike is in need of last minute attention before a big race or you need a repair in a hurry they are far more likely (and willing) to be able to help you.

7. Replace the chain regularly

Many professional cycling team mechanics replace the chain every 2,000–3,000km (1,250–1,875 mi.). This prevents damage to the cassette (rear cogs) and chainrings, meaning they will last a good year, or longer. Leaving the same chain on for months means that the next time you replace it the gears will skip and you'll have to replace the whole drive-train, which is far more expensive.

8. Lubricate

Keeping the chain and moving parts lubricated and clean, will prolong the lifespan of these expensive components. Use a quality lightweight chain lube and a bike on specific spray oil gears and brake pivots. Use a heavier waterproof oil in the winter months.

9. Keep your tyres at the recommended pressure

This cannot be stressed enough. Road tyres grip better and last well if they are run at the right pressures. They will also repel thorns, flints and glass shards. Mountain bike tyres need to be adapted for the terrain and the conditions and they also need to be pumped to suit the rider. Lighter riders can put less air in to get more grip, while heavier riders should ride fatter tyres at higher pressures to prevent pinch flats.

10. Ride in company

If all else fails and you're completely 'mechanically challenged', ride in a group. There will always be a rider with more skills than you and they will want to keep the group moving, so don't be insulted if they fix the flat for you.

What to wear

Cycling clothes are very specialized and there are many excellent fabrics that can cope with all levels of extremes that the weather can chuck at you. Ideally, you will have three cycling wardrobes:

- the basic kit
- autumn/winter
- spring/summer.

The basics

Cycling shorts

An essential – they must have a padded insert for comfort, otherwise those long rides are going to be very unpleasant.

Cycling shoes and pedal systems

A good clipless pedal system and a pair of well-fitted cycling shoes is essential for comfort, speed and safety. Before you start training seriously you need to have some!

Helmet

Always wear one. If it's cold you can wear a headband, ear warmers or cloth cap underneath.

Cycling jersey

With three rear pockets for food and essentials, a zip pocket is a good idea for keys and valuables. Typically, it's short sleeves in the summer and long in the winter – although long sleeves are a good idea when mountain biking in the summer as they offer some protection from the undergrowth.

Gloves

A good pair of gloves will not only aid grip when your hands sweat, but they offer vital protection should you take a fall – your instinct will always be to put your hands out so it's worth protecting them as much as possible.

Autumn/winter wardrobe

Winter jacket

A good quality wind and waterproof jacket will make your winter training possible and more enjoyable.

Overshoes

Essential in colder climates as they keep your feet warm and protect your shoes.

Gloves

A good pair of insulated gloves that also allow you to use the controls on your bike freely.

Long sleeves are a good idea for mountain biking as they protect your arms from the thorns and brambles in the undergrowth.

Winter tights

Tights will make your winter miles happier – they will keep you warm and have the added benefit of coming in plenty of reflective and bright colours to help you be seen in reduced visability and dark conditions.

Spring/summer wardrobe

Rain jacket

A lightweight rain jacket is ideal for carrying in your pocket and will prove invaluable on cold descents and sudden rain storms.

Leg and arm warmers

In all but the hottest weather it's advisable to wear leg or knee warmers as they keep the muscles warm and prevent any cold-induced injuries. Arm warmers can be used to make a short-sleeved top into a long sleeved one! These items are lightweight and can be easily stored.

Gloves are an essential piece of kit – for both performance and protection.

Carrying a pump and all the spares in your pockets is never ideal, but it is better to have it all just in case.

What to carry

When out training there are a few essentials you must never leave home without. Even if you ride in a group you cannot rely on others if you decide to turn back or go on alone. You need to be completely self-sufficient and prepared for all eventualities. It's a cautionary tale but the things you carry will help you get home safely and prevent any major problems, so although it sounds a bit gloomy, the advice is for the worst case scenarios – crashes are rare and bike emergencies like punctures and bits rattling loose can be easily rectified. Just be prepared!

Food

Try to approach long training rides as you would a big event. It's a good opportunity to practice eating and drinking the stuff you will when you race. Energy bars are a good idea and take up less space than cakes and bananas but long training rides may mean you run out of food – carry a little money too, so you can fuel up in an emergency.

Drink

Be sure to take two full bottles of energy drink or one of water and one of energy drink. Again, you are trying to simulate event situations and hydration is the key to top performance. Before you leave have somewhere in mind on your route to stop and fill up on your long rides.

Map

A good idea, especially if your route is a new one!

Tools

Most multi-tools have enough tool applications for all the bits on your bike. A chain tool is also a good idea, but learn how to use them – expensive multi-tools are useless if you can't use them properly.

Tubes

Always carry at least one spare tube and at least two in the winter. Also carry a puncture repair kit (emergency patches are also good) just in case you run over a hedgehog... Also carry tyre levers.

Pump

A good mini-pump is enough just to get you home, but a bigger frame fitting pump is better for longer rides when you can reach higher pressures quicker and easier. For long winter training rides a good pump is essential. Always ask other riders for recommendations and again practice pumping up your tyres with the equipment you will carry so you are confident in an emergency.

Mobile Phone

An essential safety net. If all else fails you can call for a lift home. Put an 'In Case of Emergency' number into your phone's memory, as this could be important if you have a crash.

ID

Carrying ID is a good idea, especially if you train alone. Also any medical issues you may have should be made obvious. Stitch the information into your jersey pockets. Some helmets have a form that can be filled in and stuck to the inside of your lid.

A credit card

They take up very little space and can be a life-saver if you have to buy a train ticket or pay for a cab home!

Something to put it all in...

The best place to carry this stuff is in a saddle pouch. However a phone could get wet and your ID will be harder to find, so small items and food are better carried in your jersey pockets. Wrap your phone in a small polythene bag and remember that you may sweat into food so wrap it up in tin foil. Tools, tubes and pumps are best carried on the bike. House keys should be kept safely in a cushioned place (a key can be painful if you fall on it!).

Lastly if you're riding alone tell someone how long you expect to be and where you are going – it's not always possible, but it's a good safety clause.

Carrying stuff on a mountain bike is best done in a hydration style trail bag, rather than in pockets which can snag and bounce around.

Where to ride

On-road or off-road – whatever your preference, the easiest place to finding a way into cycle sport is via your local bike shop. Good bike shops usually have a fair share of bike riders working there. Ask them who they ride with and if you can join them. They may have notices for local cycling clubs or groups and will usually be able to tell you where and when various groups meet and the type of riding that they do. Alternatively, use the websites of national organisations and hone your searches by viewing local club's websites, telephoning the local secretary for a chat, or contacting your local council who should have a list of cycling clubs and contacts in the area.

Essentially, when choosing where to ride, you have three choices:
- on-road
- off-road
- on the track.

Be prepared to embrace various disciplines. As a road rider, your bike handling will benefit from off-road riding and as an off-road rider your speed will be enhanced by riding on the road (and your body will take less of a hammering, which means you'll be able to train more). Similarly, even sprinters need an element of endurance to help them get through heats of a competition and they may not have access to a track all the time, so they will gain from riding on or off the road.

For more detailed information on the benefits of riding on the road, the track or off-road, see *Chapter 4*.

On-road

This is probably the simplest place to ride your bike and is likely to be where you have put in most of your miles so far. As a result, it is easy to forget that it can also be a pretty dangerous place, so always give consideration to other road users (see *Traffic*, below).

The road is often seen as a place for road racers only and time triallists (or commuters) – this couldn't be further from the truth. You'll see throughout this book that we recommend off-road riders take to the roads as part of their training – long roads with good surfaces are perfect for developing your endurance.

Off-road

Local woods or trails are usually the first port of call for mountain bikers. Since the beginning of mountain biking there has been much misinformation about the impact of the mountain bike on the environment. Truth is, as long as you are respectful and stick to designated bridlepaths, there's virtually no adverse environmental impact caused by riding a bike off-road.

However, purpose built mountain bike trails are on the increase, leading to some very high quality rides. These routes are often in fairly remote locations which may require a weekend of travelling to get to, so they need to be planned. But they are well worth a visit.

Wherever you ride, be sensible and do not to ride on busy public parks or paths. Find a wood or open space that isn't used too heavily by dog walkers and check that cycling is allowed there. If there are any restricted areas, do respect them. Any restrictions are usually there to protect the flora and fauna but if one or two riders are seen to flout the bye-laws, then the area is likely to become prohibited to everyone.

As well as enjoying the woods and local park lands, cyclo-cross riders can often be found training in floodlit parks and sports centres. A small circuit can provide the perfect practice ground and street lights can mean that these can be used throughout the winter. For safety reasons as well as the benefits of pushing each other a little bit harder, train with a partner or in a small group and let someone know where you are going. Local clubs and bike shops will be the best place to find new people to ride with, so go and ask their friendly advice.

On the track

Nothing does as much for cycling and the potential of young athletes as a proper, all weather, covered velodrome. However, there are far-more outdoor tracks. These are perhaps the safest place to start cycle racing as the environment is traffic-free and well-controlled. The big downside is that they can't be used in the rain and so most outdoor tracks do not have any training or racing activities scheduled over the winter months.

On road...

There are a number of benefits of track riding:

- it is a controlled environment and a safe way to practice the skills required to be a good rider, whatever your preferred discipline – there are no vehicles or rogue sheep to get in your way!
- It will help to build strength, as much of the racing is explosive and requires aggressive and assertive riding.
- coaches can keep a close eye on you and provide guidance.
- cycling with other riders helps to develop tactical knowledge.

All tracks have drop-in days and try out sessions. These are great fun. Under the supervision of a coach you'll quickly pick up the techniques to ride a fixed wheel bike and before long you'll be zipping round the bankings like a seasoned 'trackie'.

Contact a club

As with any sport, it is well worth considering taking part and training with others – it's a great help to motivation, you'll have the opportunity to learn from many riders far more experienced than you, and it's a good way to make friends with people who have similar interests. The best place to start is by joining a club.

... or off-road. Or maybe try them both – and the track.

Mountain biking has changed the face of group cycling. No longer are club rides a 'last man back buys the coffee' type of experience. Riders usually meet at a regular spot and time and the leaders will make sure that you get back to that point – some of the more experienced riders will act as riding 'marshals' to check on everyone and offer tips and advice along the way. Your local bike shop is a great place to start as many run their own regular road and mountain bike rides.

It is also well worth taking the effort to find your local cycling club. Again, ask at your local shop for your nearest club, or a few minutes on the internet will provide you with a list of clubs covering all cycling disciplines.

When to ride

Obviously, your cycling time is going to be influenced by a number of factors – not least work, family and other commitments (*see Chapter 5*). However, below are a few points to bear in mind when thinking of when to ride.

Early morning

If you have a full-time job, then the bulk of your training time is likely to be early morning or after work. For morning training, just set your alarm clock a bit earlier! Indeed, many top international riders with full-time jobs have managed to secure plenty of training time built around their working day, even if it means a two hour commute to build in the desired quantity.

There are many benefits to early morning cycling: it allows you to get the training miles out of the way early in the day, you can combine it with your work commute (thus saving travelling expense), and exercising early in the day will lift your metabolism for the rest of the day thus maximising fitness benefits.

Be sure to take a set of lights with you if you may still be out after dark or if bad weather could reduce visibility.

Lunchtime

If you are very lucky and can work in some flexi-time with your work, getting out for an hour or more at lunchtime is a great way of getting extra training time. Having riding buddies or work colleagues to meet up with will encourage you out, so try to make it a regular thing. You can manage a good workout in a 60–90 minute break from the daily grind, as long as you have the facilities for washing and bike storage.

Like all training, preparation is the key and can save time getting out on the bike and getting back to work in time for a meeting or shift. Eating lunch early (two hours before the ride) and then having a late afternoon snack will help fuel the workout. You just need to be organised. You may be able to get to a lunchtime spinning class or gym session. However, turbo training in the office is not recommended, unless you work alone!

Evening

Evening riding isn't always ideal. The traffic is often worse and people are less attentive after a long day at work. However, if there is a chaingang training ride in your area this will provide the benefit of both safety in numbers and the probability of stretching you out of your immediate comfort zone as everyone battles to avoid being the weakest link. A really hard training session can be a great way to unwind after a stressful day but these sessions are best reserved for the lighter evenings of spring and summer only.

Traffic

Traffic is a cyclist's occupational hazard. We share the roads with cars, buses, trucks, motorcyclists, horse-riders and pedestrians and their needs should always be respected just as much as ours. As a cyclist, you are more vulnerable than most other road users so discretion is always wise. Stay calm and back off, even when the other party is blatantly at fault and may have endangered you on the road.

Ride positively, about 50–100cm (2–3ft) away from the kerb to leave yourself room to move in should the need arise but still leaving room for motorists to pass you safely. Adjust this distance on busy or narrow roads. Do not obstruct other traffic unless you feel that there is not room for the two of you to be on the same spot of road, when sometimes it is better to hold your ground and prevent traffic from squeezing you into the kerb. Get out of the way as quickly as possible afterwards and give a polite 'thank you' wave when the motorist passes you. Impatient drivers may try to intimidate you by engine revving or by driving very close to you. This is a good sign not to argue with them. Road rage is far too common and can have serious, even tragic, consequences, particularly for unprotected cyclists. Do not provoke other road users with gestures or by shouting at them.

Obey the highway rules: stop at red lights and do not ride the wrong way along 'One Way' streets. Cyclists' disregard for traffic rules only antagonises other road users who may vent their frustrations on the next rider they encounter!

Always look behind and give clear and positive indication of your intended movements. Occasionally, on very busy roads, it is better to pull in to the roadside and wait for a gap in the traffic before crossing to the other side.

Cars and lorries towing trailers or caravans can be the most frightening traffic on the road. Never assume that once a vehicle has passed you that it is safe to resume your position in the road until you have checked over your shoulder. Trailers may be wider than the vehicle hauling them. Ride steadily and move a little closer to the kerb when vehicles need to pass you.

Be alert at all times. Pedestrians have an uncanny habit of appearing in the road from behind parked cars. Car doors can swing open unexpectedly. Cars may suddenly pull out into the road without signalling. Look ahead and around you at all times. Look for passengers in parked cars. Smoke from an exhaust pipe indicates an engine has just been turned on and the car is about to move. Watch for pedestrians on the pavement. Don't ride too close to the kerb or near parked cars and you will at least give yourself a nano-second or two of grace in which to take evasive action if needed. Expect the worst at all times – you will probably be correct most of the time and pleasantly surprised when you are wrong.

Careful route planning will help to reduce the incidences of meeting traffic and its associated hazards. But in sparsely populated rural areas the lack of traffic can be just as alarming. The few motorists there are may not expect to encounter other road users and may be travelling faster than they ought. Be vigilant and visible at all times. Try to have an 'escape route' to hand e.g. getting off the bike in a hurry, taking to the pavement or a nearside turn – anything that avoids impact with a fast-moving, solid vehicle is acceptable and preferable to a collision.

Weather conditions

Extremes of heat, cold, wind, fog, snow or ice can turn any ride into a potentially lethal one. Even in relatively mild climates such as the UK, conditions can change rapidly and may be life-threatening to the foolhardy or ill-prepared. For example, the top of a climb such as the Cat and Fiddle in the Peak District in the middle of England can be 5°C (41°F) cooler than Macclesfield at its foot – in this situation, it's worth carrying a lightweight gillet or rain jacket for conditions at the top and for the rapid but chilling fast swoop back down towards sea-level.

Like every other aspect of your training, a little planning can save a lot of hassle and help avoid many problems.

Leg warmers are ideal for riding in cold conditions and for warming up before races.

- Know the situation – it takes a matter of minutes to look up the latest weather forecasts, and there are many sources available (radio, internet, television, local tourist offices, newspapers, etc). Be sure that you know what conditions you are heading out in and plan your route, clothing, sun block, food and drink accordingly.

- Lighting – for training rides, especially in winter, it's worth having at least a rear LED lamp on your bike even if you expect to be home long before darkness falls, just in case you encounter low cloud or if rain makes visibility poor. Many of these lights are now made so small and lightweight some riders even use them in time trials if there is any question about visibility on the road.

A lightweight rain jacket is ideal for carrying in your pocket and will be useful for cold descents and sudden rain storms.

- Have contingency plans – even best laid plans can go awry. You may have an enforced stop due to mechanical problems, or be out for longer than anticipated if the weather turns suddenly or a headwind slows you down.
- Always carry a lightweight jacket, plenty of drink, tools and a spare tube or two, some cash and, if you're exploring new routes, a map.

Adverse weather need not hinder you, but you do need to be prepared for it.

Rain

- Rain changes the road surface, reduces braking response, decreases visibility and accelerates heat loss from the body.
- Wet roads are more slippery than dry roads.
- After a dry spell rain can bring oil, diesel and petrol spill to the road surface. Pay particular attention to this in towns and on corners. Slow down, do not take corners too fast or lean the bike over dramatically.
- Some tyre compounds cope better with wet conditions than others. Ask your dealer or cycling colleagues what they recommend for wet or greasy roads. Your own choice based on personal experience may be different. Wider tyres and lower tyre pressures are generally favoured in wet conditions to provide more traction.
- Water between the rim and brake blocks inhibits braking performance. Allow more time and distance to slow down or halt, particularly if riding fast e.g. down a hill. Use the appropriate brake blocks for your rims. Rubber or some synthetic compounds are better on aluminium rims but cork is best for carbon-fibre wheels.
- Rain washes debris into the road and water softens tyre treads, making them more susceptible to picking up flints or broken glass, leading to punctures.
- Check your tyres and brake blocks frequently and pick out any grit.
- Avoid painted lines on the road and take care at zebra crossings. They can be very slippery in the wet. Ride steadily and cross them at right angles.
- Avoid riding through puddles when you can. As well as giving you a thorough soaking, they can hide pot-holes and other hazards.
- Heat moves from warmer to colder conditions, and water conducts heat 25 times better than air. So when you get wet from rain or snow you rapidly lose body heat, especially through your head, hands and feet, so keep dry and you will remain warmer for much longer.

For guidance on cornering in wet conditions, see *Chapter 2* page 42.

Fog and mist

- The key issue about riding in fog is lack of visibility. You need to be seen by other road users so wear bright colours like red, yellow or orange and use lights.
- It's obvious, but your own vision will also be impaired, so be cautious and don't go haring into the unknown.
- Sometimes it's worth delaying your ride for an hour or two as morning fog or mist usually clears within that time (except perhaps in late autumn, when it may persist all day, in which case you're better off doing some turbo training instead).
- Fog is wet – see *Rain,* above.

Snow

- Use wide tyres and run them at lower pressures to gain more traction.
- Stay relaxed to keep better control of your bike.
- If possible, ride on new snow (provided it's not fallen on top of icy surfaces) rather than on compacted snow which will act like ice.
- Make sure you are dressed for the conditions. A hat underneath your helmet, gloves and overshoes are virtually essential.
- Off-road, with wider knobbly tyres, snow is less of a problem and can be great fun.

Ice

- If there's ice on the road, you need to avoid it. That may mean staying at home for a turbo session instead.
- Avoid applying your brakes on ice. This is a sure-fire method to lock the wheel, skid and fall – quicker than you can think.
- If necessary, get off and walk around the ice.
- If that's not possible, unclip one foot and be prepared to dab it on the ground should the bike begin to slip.
- For cyclo-cross, there are some dedicated studded ice-tyres, but most riders use mud-tyres at low pressures.
- Pedal smoothly and stay relaxed.

Wind

- Unless it's really strong, wind need not be any more than a tiring nuisance (if it's blowing in the wrong direction).
- If hazardous winds are forecast, this is another reason to stay at home and dust off the turbo trainer – unless, perhaps, you are planning a place-to-place record attempt.
- In windy areas you'll soon appreciate the benefits of adopting an aerody-namic position and riding in echelon.
- Be careful of debris flying around.
- You'll appreciate shelter of buildings or hedges, but be aware of strong gusts of wind blowing across you as you leave the shelter.
- Cold winds can soon take your body heat away, but there are plenty of windproof garments available to keep you warm.

Sun

- Sunshine may be the weather we all dream of for cycling, but it can also be a hazard.
- Always use sunblock if you expect any sunshine, and in the summer time. The sun can be surprisingly powerful even through clouds.
- Hot conditions can melt tarmac and so cause handling problems, particu-larly when steering round corners.

A good quality wind and waterproof jacket will make your winter training possible and more enjoyable.

Cycling skills

Introduction

With the basics in place, the next step is to master riding a bike. This may sound a little ridiculous – after all, as the saying goes, 'it's as easy as riding a bike'. But therein lies the problem – riding a bike is one of those skills that most of us learn at a young age and take for granted, therefore we never stop and analyse how we are doing it and whether we could do it better.

This chapter is about the skills of riding a bike. It starts off by asking you to analyse your own competencies and, by referring your answers to the skills matrix, guides you towards the cycling discipline where you may perform best (and this could well be in a very different direction from where you thought you should excel). You can also use the matrix as a method of developing the specific skills that you need to perform in a discipline that you have always wanted to try. The rest of the chapter then looks at the various skills of cycling, giving you tips and guidance on how to improve and develop.

Skills Matrix

Each cycling discipline has a unique blend of required skills that you will need in order to take part and, if it's your intention, compete. The following matrix lists the various skills and refers them to each cycling discipline – each skill is then given a rating of 1–5 depending on how important it is to the discipline in question. For example, handling skills for a would-be cross country mountain biker are vital (hence a rating of 5) whereas aerodynamics are of little importance (and get a rating of 1).

SKILLS MATRIX

	ROAD RACING	TIME TRIALLING	TRACK SPRINT	TRACK ENDURANCE	MOUNTAIN BIKE XC	MOUNTAIN BIKE DOWNHILL	CYCLO-CROSS	CYCLO-SPORTIVE
GROUP RIDING	5	1	3	4	3	1	5	3
CHANGE OF PACE	5	1	5	4	4	4	4	1
SPRINTING	4	1	5	3	4	2	4	1
ENDURANCE	4	3[1]	1	3	3	1	3	5
CLIMBING	3	2	1	1	4	1	3	3
DESCENDING	3	3	1	1	4	5	4	3
AERO-DYNAMICS	3	5	3	4	1	3	1	2
GEAR SELECTION	4	4	5	4	4	4	4	3
TACTICAL AWARENESS	5	1	5	5	3	3	4	2
HANDLING SKILLS	4	2	4	4	5	5	5	3

[1] *Depending on distance or time of event*

Group riding

We use the definition 'group riding' to cover a number of skills that are needed to be able to ride safely and effectively with other riders in close proximity.

Group riding is important in the mass start events – road racing, cross country mountain biking and cyclo-cross – where riders are together in large or small groups. Depending on which track event you do, it has greater or lesser bearing. It's not relevant to individual pursuiting but certainly is for the scratch, points, Madison, kierin and devil races, and for quite a few match sprints too.

For leisure riders, the importance of this skill depends on your preferred style, whether you want to ride in company or not. It's a useful skill to have, though, especially for those events with hundreds of entrants, or even in smaller events so that you can hook up with a few other riders of similar ability, and share the workload and some company for what can be a very long day.

It's really only the individual nature of time trialling which precludes group riding as a necessary skill, but again, it's handy to be competent at it for more interesting training sessions and if ever you ride a team time trial.

Change of pace

This encompasses the ability to accelerate very rapidly so as to: catch your rivals off guard and put distance between your bike and theirs; keep with the bunch when the pace increases; follow an attack; launch your own attack; or bridge a gap in a road race. Road races and points races on the track are notorious for the yo-yoing of speed and this is often more tiring than riding a time trial at a higher, but consistent, pace.

This is a skill typically required of the mass start events, rather than the individual disciplines, but it may be required in the closing stages of a track pursuit in order to counter your rival's pace.

Sprinting

In terms of skill, we use 'sprinting' to cover the ability to reach and maintain a very high cadence speed for a short duration of time (up to about 20 seconds). As well as match sprinting on the track and the short track time trials, this applies to the sprints or 'primes' in a road race or points race on the track and when exiting every corner in a town centre criterium. Even in the off-road disciplines of cyclo-cross and mountain biking, the initial 'gallop' from the start line often has enormous bearing on the final outcome of these events which last for an hour or two. It's also useful to be able to sprint in order to 'break the elastic' if a rider is saving their energy by following your wheel. Of course, time triallists and leisure riders will have less need to sprint and may prefer to spend their training time on other skills.

Endurance

Endurance is a relative term – it really does depend on the event. Strictly speaking, endurance should be used to cover any aerobic activity – that is any activity lasting more than 60 seconds – but, clearly, a 200km audax event demands more endurance than a 4,000m pursuit, a 10-mile time trial or an hour-long cyclo-cross race.

Aerodynamics are most important to the time triallists.

When applying the term to race disciplines, we have assumed an 'average' duration of an event:

- 2–3 hours for road races of 80–120km
- time trials of 10 and 25mi. will take a fit club cyclist about 22–25 minutes and 55–65 minutes respectively
- cyclo-cross races are usually about one hour
- cross country mountain bike races last 1–2 hours
- downhill mountain bike events are rarely more than three minutes, although this depends on the size of the mountain or hill
- most track events fall between the 200m sprint (about 10–11 seconds for elite men) to about 20–25 minutes for a 15km scratch race.

Climbing

Any uphill gradient is a climb. The need to develop your climbing abilities will depend on where you live and ride. Track riders and those who live in the flat lands may have little need or desire to work on their climbing abilities, but for anyone else climbing can be a key element in deciding whether or not they 'make the grade'. Hills invariably 'shake out' any group of riders – whether it's a club run or a mountain stage in the Tour de France. Being able to tackle hills, especially at speed, enables the best riders to put great distance between themselves and their rivals.

Descending

Gravity-assisted, descending should be a straightforward matter. However, it's surprising how descending abilities can vary from one rider to another. Being able to read the road or trail and the conditions to select the perfect line, and having confidence in your bike and your own handling skills, makes a significant difference to the manner and time in which riders descend.

Like climbing, with the exception of track riding and those in relatively flat geographical area, descending skills are relevant to all the other disciplines.

Aerodynamics

Aerodynamics are significant to all cyclists – there is no point in making a ride unnecessarily difficult. However, they are the biggest concern to time triallists and pursuit riders on the track. In the other disciplines it's more a matter of taking advantage of other riders' slipstream or adopting a lower position on the bike to present a smaller frontal area to the wind to avoid wasting energy. Below about 25kph (15mph) aerodynamics have little effect, hence their low score for the off-road activities.

Gear selection

For most cycling disciplines, you will have multiple gears so you can choose the ideal gear – perhaps even using your handlebar computer to show if you go a fraction more quickly or slow with a change of gear. But even with the combination of up to ten sprockets and two or three chainrings, you need to find the optimal gear to balance speed against fatigue. Rather than making things easier, as you may assume, the choice of 30 gears can make things a lot more difficult.

Track events using a fixed gear lie at the other extreme. Here you will have to make this selection beforehand and it's absolutely crucial to get it right for your strength and style, the track, conditions and tactics of the event.

Tactical awareness

Tactical awareness is obviously important where you are competing against others, knowing when to make a move or react to someone else. But even in individual disciplines you need a strategy for pacing yourself. For the long distance riders 'tactical awareness' extends to including plans for eating and drinking.

Handling

Handling skills cover a rider's ability to control the bike – from techniques as simple as pointing it in the direction you wish to travel or keeping the bike upright on poor surfaces, to turning a corner at speed and the special manner in which cyclo-cross riders leap off and on their bikes for obstacles. Again, this may sound like one of those skills that should rank as a 5 for every discipline but we use the term in a relative sense.

Good handling skills are essential for cyclo-cross and mountain bike riding where the terrain can dip or rise sharply, not only in front of you but also to the sides, and where the course may be strewn with obstacles. Even the sportive riders need to be able to avoid hazards on the road and deal with other riders close by from time to time. Once again, it's just the individual time triallist who can afford not to worry too much about bike handling skills – although it does help your speed (and safety) when you ride in a straight line if you can anticipate hazards and take appropriate action.

Every race situation will involve a level of tactical awareness and strategy.

Developing cycle skills

Please don't be tempted to skip over this section. Even if you feel you are complete-ly proficient in every skill that you need for your discipline, take a minute to read the following. At the very worst, you will get to smile to yourself as you confirm that you do everything as the pro riders do. At best, you may learn something that enables you to ride more safely or more quickly.

Braking

The best skill to start with is stopping or, more accurately, the ability to control your speed. It is covered in many of the skills below – descents, cornering, etc. – but it is worth a few words in its own right.

It may sound obvious, but it is a point that is often overlooked – in order to brake effec-tively you need well-maintained brakes with the levers positioned where you can oper-ate them easily. Whatever style of brakes you have, they should begin to bite when the lever has travelled about one third of its movement and be at full power by the time the lever has travelled half to two thirds of the way to the handlebar. If the lever goes beyond that, or if it touches the handlebar, you need to adjust your brakes.

Braking is also dependent on the amount of traction between the tyre and the ground and will vary with speed and ground surface – whether it's smooth, rough or loose, dry or wet. Downhill mountain bikers need the most powerful brakes as they descend at breakneck speeds on heavy, gravity-friendly bikes. Hence they use motorcycle-style disc brakes so they can maintain their pace and leave braking to the last fraction of a second. The techniques employed are much the same, though, whether you are time triallist with only one roundabout to negotiate (albeit less exaggerated) or a mountain biker threading your way down a muddy slope.

Find a stable position

You need a stable position on your bike. Hold your hands wide and cover the brake levers. Keep your head up and look where you are going at all times. Your front brake is more powerful and has more effect on the bike's steering than the rear, so apply a little more power to the front brake. If you are travelling fast, stop pedalling and move your feet and cranks into a horizontal position. Straighten your arms and slide your body weight backwards over the saddle as you brake to prevent the bike from tipping forwards.

Off-road riders may well find themselves hanging over the back of the saddle on steep descents. To help slow down from high speeds, sit more upright to present a bigger area to the wind.

Brake before the corner

Brake before a corner, not in it. Keep looking where you want to go. If you find your-self travelling too fast through the corner, feather the rear brake. If the bike begins to slide out, ease off the brake and adjust your body weight to travel with the rear wheel. Applying the front brake will cause the bike to move upright again – useful if you've misjudged a corner and need to re-align the bike in a new direction.

BRAKING CHECKLIST

- Hold handlebars low and wide with fingers over brake levers.
- Know which lever operates your front and rear brakes
- Keep your head up and look where you are going
- Avoid snatching at the brakes – instead apply steady pressure to the levers
- Apply fractionally more power to the front brake
- Hold the handlebars straight and avoid turning when braking
- Stop pedalling and shift body weight back to help maintain traction and balance
- Allow more stopping distance when travelling fast or when on poor surfaces

Braking in a group

When riding in a group, avoid sudden braking. If you do have to slow down, use your rear brake. This will telegraph to the rider behind what you are doing, rather like the brake lights on cars.

It is better to adjust your speed by drifting into a space out of the slipstream of the rider in front. Better still, keep an eye on what's going on ahead and you should be able to anticipate most situations before anyone needs to take emergency action. On downhill sections, give yourself a little more room between yourself and the rider ahead.

Braking in adverse conditions

Allow more braking time and expect to brake harder in wet conditions. It will take a wheel revolution or two before your rims clear of water. Beware too of slippery conditions and keep the bike as upright as possible when braking.

Maintenance

Check your cables and brake blocks regularly, especially after wet rides or when riding in mountainous areas, and replace them as soon as they appear worn. Off-road riders will need to replace brake blocks or pads quite frequently as the extra dirt from the trails will act like sandpaper and rapidly wear the blocks (and rims).

Pedalling

Another contender for most obvious statement in this book, but again one that needs to be made as it is often overlooked: pedalling is key to riding a bicycle. In order to compete in any cycling discipline or, indeed, to be able to ride for fun, you need to be able to pedal efficiently. However, defining what constitutes the ideal technique is a difficult thing to pin down because pedalling is highly individual; a rhythm like a personal cycling blueprint.

Cadence

There have been numerous studies about the ideal cadence – the speed at which you pedal, typically measured in revolutions per minute (rpm) – for cycling, and almost invariably the scientists have come up with figures far lower than those actually used by cyclists. This may be because they use people not trained as cyclists in their tests and non-cyclists tend to prefer a cadence of about 60rpm, close to the number of paces they take when walking. In contrast, most experienced cyclists keep to a figure of at least 80rpm, and often closer to 100rpm.

Finding the cadence that works best for you and making the correct choice of gear selection lies at the heart of developing your pedalling technique. If you are in the same gear as the next rider and you can pedal faster, then you will go faster. However, if you do not have the strength to pedal as big a gear as your opponent, his or her lower cadence may prove more effective than your higher cadence. To some degree, whether you are a twiddler of low gears or a grinder of big gears depends on the proportion of fast-twitch and slow-twitch fibres in the composition of your muscles. This means that we all have our own optimum cadence, but this can be altered with training to recruit more of the appropriate fibres.

This rider displays textbook braking position on a corner.

COUNTING CADENCE

You do not need a cadence meter to measure your pedalling rate. Just use your watch and count the number of times one leg pushes down in a minute.

CRANK SIZE

Your crank size should be related to your pedalling style and gear size. If you are aiming to turn a small gear very rapidly, then you'll find that smaller cranks are easier to use – as the cranks travels less distance for each revolution and so can be spun quicker. On the other hand, grinding a big gear requires more leverage and a longer crank will prove beneficial.

Here are some 'rule of thumb' sizes:

· track riding – 165mm cranks are common to help riders deal with rapid accelerations and changes in pace (plus they provide extra clearance needed for steeply banked – particularly indoor – tracks)
· time trials – long, 175–180mm cranks are often favoured to help overcome some unfeasibly large gears
· tour riding – 170mm cranks are usually used to cope with the lower gears tourists need to move them and their luggage over all sorts of terrains
· road racing – 172.5mm or 175mm cranks are usually preferred as a good compromise between the short cranks of the track riders and ultra-long cranks of the time triallists
· off-road riding – 172.5mm or 175mm cranks are the norm, as it's almost impossible to pedal fast and smoothly over uneven terrain, so the extra leverage is useful for coping with the inevitably slightly slower off-road cadences (and anything longer would be likely to catch on rocks or roots).

(See *Chapter 3* for further information on muscle fibres.)

Pushing a comfortably high cadence during training will develop the more efficient slow-twitch muscle groups and burn fat more quickly than bashing about in bigger gears and lower cadences. This is why you rarely see experienced riders using the big chainrings in the winter or when training – even at a very high speed you will see pro riders 'spinning' in the smaller gears and trying to maintain a high leg speed.

FAST TWITCH AND SLOW TWITCH MUSCLES

Each type of muscle fibre is recruited at different stages of a bike ride – when this happens is determined to a large extent by the type of rider you are and your level of fitness. For example, most rides (anything over a minute) will require predominantly slow-twitch fibres, but sprinting or other intense efforts such as climbing a short, steep hill will recruit more fast-twitch fibres. Of course, if you do not naturally have a prevalence of fast-twitch fibres and haven't trained for explosive efforts, you'll not be able to recruit many fast-twitch fibres.

However, as a general rule:

· the higher the gear, the slower the cadence, which means more torque is required from your muscles resulting in the recruitment of fast-twitch muscle fibres as they are capable of producing more force than slow-twitch fibres – the downside being that they use up far more glycogen (muscle energy)
· lower gears moved at a quicker cadence generally employ slow-twitch muscles fibres, which lack brute power but do have the ability to perform for a longer duration.

This basic rule is followed through to racing too – pushing big gears is okay, you just need to be going fast enough to keep the cadence high. In a race situation 'spinning' at a high cadence uses the energy-efficient slow-twitch fibres throughout a race, leaving your fast-twitch fibres fresh for the maximum effort sprint for the line.

And if you still need convincing... Lance Armstrong has proved that higher cadences are effective for long, steep climbs on the road. Although there is not a lot new in his techniques (many climbers adopt high cadences) he has certainly shown that it is possible to put a huge amount of power down, even in low gears, and provide devastating attacks from high cadences. Compare Armstrong to the 'big gear' climbing Jan Ullrich and you immediately see the contrast – Ullrich's big gear, slow cadence suits him better but it also means he can't accelerate quickly and, therefore, is slower to react. Climbers work very hard on their ability to spin up a low gear on an extreme slope, it's their only chance to catch out and hurt the flat racers. (See *Climbing*, below.)

'Souplesse'

This is the French word used by cycling coaches to refer to the ability to pedal in a fluid style almost effortlessly. Fundamentally, it is about finding the right cadence for your style and cycling discipline – only by turning the right gear at the right speed can you find a smooth and efficient style.

So is there an ideal cadence? In short: no, it's down to the individual. But as a general figure to aim for, these days a cadence 85–95rpm is recognised as the target cadence zone for pedalling.

Tour de France climbing specialists and mountain bike racers will climb at a very high cadence of around 95rpm+ and sprinters can reach 140–160rpm at top speed. Whatever riding they are doing it's pretty rare that competitive cyclists ever drop below 80rpm, ever. However 'new' cyclists will often start off pushing much bigger gears than they need to, believing that they can provide them with the speed they need to keep up and the ability to ride further. Nothing could be further from the truth.

Gearing

Gearing has a major influence on cadence (see also the sections on *Climbing* and *Sprinting*, below). The main thing to bear in mind is that the gears a pro rider can 'spin' are far higher than the average club rider, simply because they travel a lot faster (that's their job) – but they too will concentrate their Zone One and Zone Two rides spinning low gears (see *Chapter 5* for more training zones). It is a very good thing that chainset manufacturers have recently realised this and introduced 'compact' road chainsets with no more than 50 teeth on the chainring instead of the ubiquitous 53 tooth chainrings which are only of use to racing cyclists on the road. So don't get bogged down and be tempted to sling the chain onto the big ring and little sprocket to churn a massive gear. Aim to remain comfortable and concentrate on making effortless pedal strokes – let 'souplesse' become your mantra.

Road Gearing

Chainrings for road bikes come in some huge sizes – 53-tooth chainrings offer big gears and are designed for riders pushing 35kph (22mph) and over. Anything slower than this and you should be using the smaller 39 tooth chainring. However, you could consider changing to a 50-tooth chainring in the winter to ensure that you don't over-do it when you need to be going a little more slowly. At the other extreme, some coaches have been known to take the big chainring off their riders' bikes during the off season to encourage them to spin lower gears – you can follow this lead by adjusting your front derailleur limit screws so the temptation to get on the big ring is removed.

Whichever size chainring you use, be sure that it matches your aspirations and reality. A 53-tooth chainring is no use to someone who rides long audax or sportive rides at a maximum average speed of around 30 kph (18mph) – they would be much better served with a 50-tooth or smaller chainring. Slower riders might benefit from a 46 or even 44 outer ring. Coupled with a 12-tooth top sprocket (which is unlikely to be used too frequently) this still gives a top gear of 8.19m (103.5in.) which is more than enough for most racing situations!

Triple chainsets have been used to great effect for years by those in the know who live in the Pyrenees, the Alps or even the hilly areas of Britain, and they are also well suited to touring, as the low gears help to manage heavy loads up long or steep climbs. Although this gives you a wide range of gears to choose from, when you are in the smallest gears it can feel like you are churning butter and not actually making much progress. At the end of the day you still need to press on the pedals.

CHAINLINE

If you are to pedal efficiently, it follows that you need an efficient drive train. This is all down to gear selection and avoiding extreme chain angles, which will slow you down and will increase the wear on the chain, gears and the sprockets.

The most effective chainline will be a straight line from the chainring to the sprocket. In other words, the outer chainring is best used with the smaller (outboard) sprockets and the inner chainring is best used with the larger (inboard) sprockets. If you are using a triple chainset, the chain will probably comfortably reach both the smallest and largest sprockets but it may foul the outer chainring (depending on the chainring sizes, frame geometry and length of bottom bracket axle). So, again, it may be necessary to avoid the smallest sprockets.

If you do find yourself frequently wanting to use 'awkward' gears, consider buying different chainring and sprocket combinations.

Good maintenance will also help – a clean chain and sprockets and lightly-oiled gear components will last longer and spin more effectively.

The net result: you will go faster.

Mountain Bike Gearing

Triple chainsets provide numerous gear ratios for tackling steep climbs and bowling along wind-assisted flats. (In reality, few riders pedal down quick descents but instead usually reward themselves by freewheeling.) A front chainring with between 44 and 50 teeth is sufficient for anyone using a triple chainset. Choose a middle ring 8–12 teeth smaller and an inner ring a further 8–12 teeth smaller (if possible) and you'll have a range of gears to tackle pretty much anything. Tourists with luggage and mountain bikers will probably want a wide range of sprockets (up to a 28–32 largest sprocket) whereas sportive and audax riders will usually prefer closer-spaced sprockets (up to maximum of 23 or 27 teeth).

Perhaps it's inexperience but many mountain bikers do tend to over-gear on the flat and downhill sections in the quest for further speed and then spin too low a gear on the steeper uphill sections. The result is very inefficient pedalling styles and bad habits. Even off-road it's far better to adopt a more suitable gear that can be pedalled at a more efficient cadence of 80–90rpm.

The slightly smaller (26in.) wheels combined with chainrings in the region of 46–34–24 and a wide range of sprockets (usually up to 28–32 teeth) should provide enough gears to tackle all but the most difficult of terrain.

For downhilling, riders rely on pedalling at very high cadences for just a few seconds at a time. A single chainring is often sufficient, with its size dependent on the length and technicality of the gradient. A long, easy descent might be tackled with very large gear whereas something more technically demanding will require a lower gear for better acceleration past each turn, obstacle or change in terrain.

Time trialling

Pedalling faster is essential if you want to get a personal best. Many time trial veterans use inappropriately large gears, pushing massive chainrings of 54 or 55 teeth and 'straight-through' (one-tooth increments) cassettes like 11–19. These gears are really only going to help you go faster if you are already going at over 50kph (31mph) – and if you can do that for more than 40kms (25mi.) you'll be looking for a pro contract, not ways to improve your efficiency. A far more sensible approach would be to use the gears available to maintain a target cadence which is consistent throughout your training and racing.

Fixed wheel riding

Track riders develop a fluid pedalling style, the result of countless thousands of revolutions on a fixed gear. If you live in a city or in an area with flat roads, fixed gear riding is perfect for winter training and unless you live in a very hilly area can be great fun. It's also better for icy roads as the braking can be done very smoothly via the transmission. Remember that if you ride a fixed wheel bike on the road you still have to have a front brake, though there's no harm in having a rear brake too. A gear of 5.15–5.95m (65–75 inches) is ideal for training or club rides on the road.

Track training sessions will improve leg speed and also encourage fluid pedalling – coached sessions are a great idea as it's easy when someone is telling you what to do and predicting the interval or sprint session (it also makes you work harder than you would on your own). The choice of gear will vary depending on the disciplines you ride, the size and surface of the track. It's worth speaking to a local coach or riders to find out their recommendations for each track. Loosely, the top pursuit riders are now using big gears and sacrificing a quick start for greater speed later in the event, whereas sprinters use smaller gears for better acceleration and rely on their ability to pedal at very high cadences.

Cyclo-cross

Courses have generally become faster and more rideable in recent years than the old 'cross-country running with a bicycle' events of cross's early years. As a consequence, top riders may be seen sporting gears not dissimilar to many road bikes. That's all very well for them, but for the average club rider tackling local league events, lower gears are far more appropriate. An outer chainring of 46–50 teeth is quite sufficient. Coupled with an inner ring of 36–39 and wide cassette of 12 or 13–27 or 29, you will be able to ride up many slopes but if there's anything more severe on the course, you simply get off, shoulder the bike and run up the slope.

Developing your technique

Here are a few drills which you can adopt to improve your pedalling technique.

Fixed-wheel bikes

We have mentioned these above, but it is worth reiterating. Riding a fixed wheel bike either on the track or the road will certainly improve your technique. A staccato pedalling motion will cause a fixed wheel bike to alternately surge forward and slow so you need to keep your pedalling action as fluid as possible.

Riding rollers (not turbo trainers) also requires, and helps to develop, a smooth pedalling technique.

Group riding

Try following the cadence of the group of riders you are riding with, as they will generally be led by an experienced rider. Following this lead will help you find your natural speed and also help you maintain the pace. Watch what gear they have selected (ask them if you're not sure) or count their pedal revolutions. At first you may feel a little uncomfortable and it may seem like you are bouncing around a bit, but stick with it. You are trying to develop muscles that you are not used to engaging and this will take a while.

Studio cycling classes

Studio cycling (which goes by the names Spinning and RPM, and many other variations) is introducing a huge audience to the joys of cycling. These sessions are a great idea for competitive cyclists too as they can offer a break from training alone and also provide a useful interval session without having to plan exactly what you intend to do. Many spinners are finding that they are fit enough to start cycling and they have a head start as they have learned that fast cadences burn fat and develop cycling muscle groups. With a good instructor they can also be much more fun than a chaingang in the rain.

Interval sessions

Intervals on a turbo trainer can improve technique and encourage better pedalling speed when racing or riding. Use 6–10 shorter intervals of 30–60 seconds at a very high cadence (120+rpm) with a short two-minute recovery intervals in between. This can also be used on a day off, just to keep your legs fresh. (See *Chapter 5* for more on turbo trainers.)

Motor pacing

This is only for the experienced rider – it involves following a motorbike or moped. Obviously you need to do this type of training in a safe environment (on a track is best), but this training technique enables you to spin a fast cadence on a bigger than usual gear and at a far faster speed. Track 'Dernys' are popular in Six Day track events and allow fast racing, but also superb training for track racers who want to pedal at over 50kph (30mph.) It's the hardest workout you can get, and it will improve you as a cyclist too as there are techniques and tactics you will pick up into the bargain.

Greg Lemond, Tour de France winner and World Champion (the first American to do both), was known to use motor pacing as a way of simulating the high speed of the peloton. For hours he would follow a small moped at over 50kph. This meant he could push a big racing gear and still 'spin' his legs enough to train the slow-twitch muscle groups. Many riders will ride for many hours like this and finally 'break away' from, or ride alongside, the motorbike and 'recruit' the fast-twitch muscles when they are suitably fatigued – thus simulating race situations perfectly.

Riding on cobbles requires every ounce of your cycling skill – especially if they are a bit slippery!

Cornering

Training to be better at cornering is essential for road racing cyclists, mountain bikers and for those wanting to pick up speed for mountainous challenge rides. Being a better bike handler will gain you bike lengths over your rivals and when riding towards a finish line this can create the difference between winning and just being placed. But, above all, cornering safely is an essential skill as it's rare that you fall off going in a straight line.

The skills for cornering broadly fall into two categories: on-road and off-road.

Cornering basics for the road

Professional riders spend many months on training camps and technical rides in mountains and during some awful weather, factors which all add up to make them the finest bike riders in the world. So if you're a bit sketchy on the corners, get some practice time built into your training and think about what you are doing wrong. Like most techniques, it's a process and there are a few pointers that will make you a better rider, no matter how much (or little) nerve you have.

Approaching the corner you need to brake and get your body low on the bike to lower your centre of gravity.

The inside line is shorter and quicker than the outside, so you can gain an advantage by taking the quickest route.

Look for the exit line of the corner, and if riding on the open road, keep to your side of the road on the entry to the corner.

The approach

Although you might know what you're doing, others around you may not, so as you approach the corner check around you for movement of traffic or other riders. If you are confident the road is clear then move out towards to the middle of the road. This will dramatically reduce and improve your cornering angle and give you more width to negotiate the corner. The greater your entrance angle on the approach then the more difficult cornering becomes.

Brake in plenty of time

When you know a corner is approaching, cover the brake levers and start to reduce some of the speed. Your biggest cornering problem is approaching too fast and locking up the brakes in a moment of panic. Take your time and brake early – it's far better to have to let go of the brakes a bit than have to grab harder.

Ride on the drops

Cornering is often a lot easier in the drop position on your handlebars. You have easier access to your brakes, the arms become more relaxed (keep them bent), your weight is lower and is easier to shift in this position. The lower centre of gravity also means you can go faster, more safely.

Anticipate the gear change

Change to a lower gear just before the corner. This should be a gear that you can comfortably exit the corner on. It's no good pedalling into a corner on 53x12, forgetting to change gear and then grinding almost to a halt as you attempt to accelerate out the other side.

Pedal around the corner

Soft pedalling can actually help your balance as you corner around sweeping bends and extreme acceleration can throw the bike upright and kick the back wheel away from the bike. Always keep a consistent speed and pressure on the pedals.

THE PRINCIPLES OF CORNERING

The five golden rules of cornering:
- Keep your head up
- Eyes focused on the exit point
- Inside foot up, pressing weight onto the outside foot
- Hands covering the levers but not braking hard
- Relax and enjoy yourself – you'll go a lot faster

Try not to brake whilst cornering, but do 'cover' the brake levers just in case.

Shift your weight

When you are a few metres away from the corner, lift up the inside leg (the leg on the corner side) so the pedal is vertical ('at 12 o'clock'). This will improve your balance and weight distribution whilst cornering and it will stop you from grounding your pedal on the road. Distribute your weight so that it pushes down through your outside leg – this helps balance and improves tyre grip, forcing the tyres into the road. Stay relaxed and loose in your upper body – stiffening up makes the bike drift and you will start to panic and brake too hard.

Off the brakes

The best riders will never brake on the corner itself, so if you are trying to get quicker aim not to touch your brakes – cover them but resist the temptation to pull on them. By braking on the corner itself you will ruin your cornering line and end up with further problems. Remember, all the braking should have been done before the corner, allowing you to smoothly freewheel the full way round.

Keep your head up

The usual mistake is to look about two metres ahead of the front wheel, which prevents you from taking a smooth line through the corner. Keep your head up, with your eyes parallel to the horizon and look through the apex of the corner towards the point at which you want to exit. This naturally keeps you on track and heading towards where you are looking. If you look away from this line you will drift in that direction as a result. It's all about concentration.

Look towards the exit of the corner and put all your weight onto the outside leg – this will push more weight through the tyres and increase grip.

Exit the corner

On the exit of the corner, do not straighten the bike up too soon – be smooth and do it gradually. Stay in your cornering position (on the drops) until you have fully negotiated the corner. Don't pedal too soon or you'll simply whack your pedal on the road. As the bike starts to right itself you can press on the pedals again and push on.

Once out of the corner, look towards the next bend. On a series of sweeping Alpine style bends you can practise this technique and really get good at railing through the turns. Accelerating is always best done at the exit of the bend and as the bike starts to right itself. Sprinting out of corners is an essential technique for road racing as you fight to stay in contact with a peloton that speeds up at every opportunity.

Wet roads

No one enjoys riding in wet conditions. But if you are willing and able to push your tyres to the maximum, wet roads can still provide plenty of grip. The big difference from dry conditions is that spilt diesel oil, mud or gravel washed into the road can turn it into a skid pan when it rains. These hazards aren't always obvious as you fly into a bend and can therefore throw up some nasty shocks.

By following these steps – and with a bit of confidence and self-belief – you will be able to corner with ease in wet conditions.

- Look further ahead down the road – riding head down will just mean you'll not notice the hazards until you're on top of them. Smooth tarmac is usually the slippery stuff, so head for rougher areas (but only if it is safe to).
- Keep pushing your weight through the pedals and stay relaxed – this will help the tyres 'bite' through the water to happily adhere to the road.
- If your bike does skip a bit, don't brake hard – if you are relaxed you are more likely to be able to 'soak up' the skid and the bike will find grip again more quickly.
- Don't lean the bike as much as in the dry and take a wider entry and exit line.
- Run your tyres at 10% less pressure than normal.

ICE

Ice is an incredibly unpredictable surface to ride on and best avoided altogether (unless perhaps you're riding cyclo-cross in the winter). If you have to ride in extremely cold conditions, the rules are pretty simple:

- Keep the bike as upright as you can.
- Under no circumstances brake on a patch of ice.
- Relax and stay loose on the bars.

Time trials can be won and lost by hundredths of seconds, so quick cornering can win races. Lance Armstrong shows his skill.

Off-road cornering

Mountain bikers are usually pretty good at riding corners. They get plenty of practice riding tight, twisty singletrack and repetitive laps of cross-country race tracks with hundreds of obstacles and turns. But there's always room to improve – being better at cornering will gain you seconds into every corner, which can amount to minutes by the end of a long race.

Riders like Michel Rassmussen, Santiago Botero and Cadel Evans have all crossed over from the mountain bike circuit to riding at the Tour de France and Giro d'Italia. Some of these guys can really fly downhill and their cornering technique is second to none. How do they do it? Simple: practice, experience, talent and nerve.

Due to the nature of the surfaces you're riding over, cornering physics change very slightly when hitting the dirt, although the principles are much the same. You still need to follow the basics outlined above, but you have the added benefit of being able to use skidding or sliding to get through corners without loosing valuable momentum.

Sliding a corner

If you can, avoid sliding a corner as this can rip up the trail and accelerate erosion. But on maintained race trails it's a perfectly legitimate way to negotiate a turn.

On the road you would aim to move out wide for a corner and then cut across the apex and exit wide. But off-road the terrain rarely allows you to do this. If you are approaching too fast or discover the radius of the corner is tighter than expected, or you have to change your line because of rocks, roots, ditches or other obstacles on your ideal line, you may find you have to slide your wheels to help turn more quickly.

Moving your body around the bike has a massive influence on steering and the handlebars are used to fine tune these movements. Unless you're on a bermed corner (with the camber helping your turn) you'll have to lean and steer the bike.

Stay relaxed with your arms slightly bent and look where you want to go. Select your exit gear as you approach the corner and, keeping your body fairly upright, lean the bike into the corner, pressing your weight down on the outside pedal and the inside of the handlebars. Keep your body low and lean forwards to maintain some weight on the front wheel.

Approach the apex and then apply the brakes until the rear wheel locks and begins to skid. Release the brake as soon as the wheel stops turning and take the widest line out of the curve.

Straighten up out of the turn, shifting your weight back to the centre of the bike and pedal – out of the saddle if necessary – to regain your speed. This move takes practice, so try it on a safe piece of ground before using it in earnest.

If one side of the trail is obviously more solid and useable than the other, use it. That will be the quicker and safer route to take. If you have to dab a foot, unclip from the pedal as you approach the corner. Bring your leg forward, bend at the knee and point your heel down and your toes up. Let your foot skim above the ground – you'll lose speed if you dab when you don't need to, but it might just save you from wiping out and more serious consequences.

CYCLO-CROSS

Riding off-road on a racing bike with skinny tyres isn't as dumb as it first appears. Although a cross bike is no match for a mountain bike on technical downhills it is superb for fast, flat racing. In the wet a cross bike will bite through mud and find firmer grip underneath.

This discipline was initially designed for road riders to improve technique and winter fitness. It also helps you to sharpen skills that can be applied both to mountain biking and on the road. You will learn how to handle a bike in extreme conditions. But, best of all, it's in a safe, traffic-free environment. And it's (sort of) fun.

Mountain bikers also benefit from skills of cyclo-cross – in addition to handling skills, getting on and off in a hurry and running with a shouldered bike are techniques regularly used in both disciplines.

Off-camber cornering

Off-camber cornering can be particularly challenging as you are fighting gravity, try-ing to keep your momentum and negotiate the corner. Look where you want to go and keep pressing your weight into the outside pedal. A foot-out style will help counter the camber and keep your torso relaxed to absorb any trail shock and make steering easier.

Front braking

Braking hard on the front brake is best saved for the entry to the corner. The front wheel still needs to rotate so pull the brake lever gradually and softly to let the wheel rotate as much as possible. You don't want your front wheel to lock up – if it does, release the brake immediately or your wheel will start to slide. Straighten your arms and shift your weight backwards over the saddle as you apply the brake.

Poor weather conditions

Riding in adverse conditions is half the appeal of off-road riding to many people – mud and ice can turn a good trail into a great one. However, it's not always what you are looking for and there are some things to bear in mind when you are faced with these conditions.

It is exhilarating to ride trails in the snow and cold conditions. The wider tread of mountain bike tyres and the usually rough ground underneath makes light work of icy conditions. Indeed, frost can turn a usually muddy ride into a fast, dry and dusty blast.

When riding in excessively muddy or wet conditions there are a few points to bear in mind:

- Ride at the outside edge of the trail – grass is far 'grippier' than mud.
- Standing water can mean that there's some hard trail underneath and it can also serve to clear some mud from the tyres – but it can also camouflage hidden depths, so approach with caution.
- Clean off the mud from the side walls of your tyres as you ride – this will give you more cornering grip when you hit the drier ground.
- There are two schools of thought about tyre pressures – some riders run their tyres at a higher pressure to assist cutting through to harder ground, whereas others use much lower pressures to allow the tyre to spread out and get more grip.
- Narrower tyres with well spaced square knobs cut through mud better and provide more clearance around the frame.

Climbing

Like it or loathe it, if you ride a bike you are going to have to go up hills at some point. Whether you are riding Alpine climbs or rolling open country roads, both present a completely different set of challenges and require an equally different set of techniques.

Horses for courses

How you tackle a climb will depend on three things:

- the type of climb – whether it is short and sharp or a long drag
- your fitness – we'll look at this later in the book (see *Chapter 3*)
- your predisposition to being a climber – a rider with a larger mass needs more power to take him uphill. Big, powerful riders may be able to blast their way up the short, sharp climbs but on long ascents lasting more than a few minutes their size will work against them and they can easily lose significant time to more slightly-built riders who tend to have less absolute power but a better power-to-weight ratio.

A fluid style and appropriate gearing makes climbing a lot less painful.

Not all great climbers are small. Miguel Indurain and the great Eddy Merckx are both examples of 80kg (176lb) riders who managed to win the Tour de France where it matters, in the mountains. Lance Armstrong (Tour winner 1999-2005) and his rival Jan Ullrich (Tour winner in 1997 and with arguably more claim to the title of 'eternal second' than Raymond Poulidor) are both over 70kg (154lb). Perhaps the largest rider in the current Pro-peloton is Magnus Backstedt – the Swedish powerhouse is in the region of 90kg (198lb) and yet he can still stay with the rest of the non-climbers in the biggest mountain stages of the Tour de France.

So how does this happen? It's all about power-to-weight ratios and also how your body copes with sustained intensity of effort. Some of us are better at this than others – and this is due to a combination of training and genetics.

A kilo of weight saved from your body is worth far more than any weight you can save off your bike. There is a reason that skinny, slight Spanish climbers go faster in the hills than big Belgian rouleurs. So before you rush off and spend a small fortune on the latest carbon wheels or titanium frame, think about it. Did you really need that ice cream?

Practice

So how do you improve your chances in the mountains (or hills)? Simple really: ride in them. If you are a poor climber then you probably avoid hills in training. Well, don't. Get into the hills as much as is possible and ride them regularly. This will allow you to try out many of the techniques outlined below but it will also enable you to find your preferred cadence (see *Pedalling*, above).

Don't worry about your pace initially. Focus on your mindset and work on developing the attitude that hills are not a problem. Over time your confidence will increase and you will get stronger – not only will this improve your climbing, you will also see benefits of this extra power in other areas of your cycling.

Lance Armstrong made high cadence climbing one of the keys to his success.

As you get stronger, set yourself targets. Ride some sections harder and faster. Ride the top half of the hill faster than the lower section. Where races finish at the top of a hill (and many do – it makes the judges' jobs much easier) you need to be in contention at the end. Interval training will produce the necessary physical adaptations (see *Chapter 5*).

You can also start to 'play' on long climbs: riding hard at race pace, easing slightly and then going hard again. This is a form of interval training but without the full recovery periods usually associated with this type of exercise. It helps to cope with attacks and surges in speed from other riders.

Where possible, practise on the hills you will use in competition, noting landmarks where you can make attacks, and gauge your efforts. If this is not possible then make sure that you vary the hills that you use in training so that you can develop the skills and technique to take on different situations.

The professional approach

Keeping the cadence high has been the latest craze since Lance Armstrong re-invented the quick-pedalling style. Keeping a pace over 75rpm is preferred, because any lower and you'll be doing some muscle damage on long and steep hills (see *Pedalling*, above).

Away from the professional circuit there's a popular approach to climbing, 'Oh, there's a hill coming so I'll change gear as the climb progresses and that way it'll get easier as the climb goes on'. Multiple gears have allowed riders to climb the highest mountains and reach places that cyclists previously never dream of reaching. However, gears are a bit of a cheat. They allow you to take it a little too easy and approach things from a more mechanically assisted angle (which is actually a good thing to avoid serious muscle damage).

The number of gears available on modern bikes supports this approach, encouraging riders to start in a high gear and change lower and lower as the climb progresses. This technique makes sense on one level – the steeper the slope, the lower the gear required. But to the best climbers hills are a head game – they are a psychological challenge, just as much as they are a physical one.

Sure, weight and strength do come into it, but the gamble of when to up the pace and attack or just increase the speed gradually is the key when competing with others. The greatest climbers can bluff their opponents and play with them with faux attacks and by slowing the pace. If you are up to it and can cope with the changes in tempo, you can really upset riders who are already at their limit.

Two masters of this have been the Italians Marco Pantani and Claudio Chiappucci – it's worth watching video of them at their peak as they show how easy it can be. They may make it look easy, but they hurt just the same. As Greg Lemond once famously said about attacking hills: 'It doesn't hurt any less, it just gets done faster.'

GEAR RATIOS

Like virtually everything about a bicycle, the gears are very simple. The chainwheel drives the sprockets on the rear wheel via a chain and the size (shown by the number of teeth) of the chainwheel or cog dictates the size of the gear.

For example, a 52t (teeth) chainwheel is four times larger than a 13t sprocket. Thus one turn of the chainwheel will turn the sprocket – and so turn the wheel – four times. A 26t chainwheel is only two times the size of the 13t sprockets, so if this combination was used the wheel would turn only twice with one revolution of the chainwheel. The mathematics shows that a 52t chainwheel and 26t sprocket would result in exactly the same size gear.

Racing bikes tend to be fitted with an outer chainwheel of 52t or 53t, combined with an inner one of 42t or 39t, and a rear cassette of up to 10 sprockets usually ranging from 12t up to 21t or 23t, depending on the terrain. The one-tooth difference means riders can find precisely the right gear for any situation. Hillier races demand larger sprockets and a wider range of gears than those required for flatter races.

Mountain bikes and touring bikes are invariably fitted with triple chainsets to provide an even wider range of gears to cope with difficult terrain or climbing when loaded down with luggage. The extra chainring not only helps to widen the range of gears but also provides some intermediate gears to avoid uncomfortably large gaps or 'jumps' between each one. Mountain bike chainsets usually have outer chainrings of between 44t–46t, middle chainrings of 32t–36t and an inner chainring of 22t–26t, and as such are ideal for touring use. Riders from both disciplines tend to choose wide ratio cassettes with the largest sprocket often 28t or even up to a massive 34t for an ultra-low gear.

Audax and sportive riders usually take the middle ground. Compact chainsets with using 50t–36t or 48t–34t are now common, combined with sprockets from 12t or 13t to 25t or 29t, according to the rider's preference and the terrain they are covering.

Technique and terrain

Long Alpine-style climbs are perhaps the biggest challenge for any rider. Riders who can't climb will never win a Grand Tour. It's a challenge that many riders will never face, but the long 20km–30km (12.5–20mi.) mountain climbs command total respect and can only be taken on with preparation and specific training. That said, even though few of us will take these climbs on, there are plenty of lessons to be learned.

Position on the bike

For long climbs, sit back in the saddle with your hands wide on the tops of the handlebars or brake hoods. This will help your breathing. Find a comfortable gear, and get into a rhythm with your cadence at a reasonable level (70–90rpm). Of course, if you can pedal a higher gear you will ascend faster and scare your rivals with your strength.

On very long climbs, you may find it beneficial to press harder every other pedal stroke in order to conserve energy. For example, count 1-2-3, 1-2-3 with the pedals, left-right-left, right-left-right or you might find this easier counting up to 5, 7 or 9 – just keep it to an odd number and you'll keep the effort going.

Short climbs create few problems for top road riders.

Pacing

When taking on long climbs – and 'long' in this case is relative to you and your abilities – pace yourself. Start the hill at a comfortable pace that you know you can sustain to the top. If you are riding in a group, let the quicker riders disappear as they attack one another. Don't be tempted to ride at their pace, ride your own race. If possible, use a heart rate monitor (HRM) to keep an eye on your effort levels and keep within your target zones – fluctuations due to temperature, anxiety, hydration levels, etc. make it difficult to compare rides on different days.

As the hill progresses, you'll probably find that many of those who went off too fast early on will start to appear on the horizon as they have expended their energy and are digging deeper than they needed to. It's always far better to make progress on climbs rather than drift off the back because you have pushed on too early and over-reached. Once you're cooked and you've produced an overload of lactic acid, it may take many minutes to recover and start to climb consistently again, so listen to your legs and you if they hurt, back off.

Get ahead

On shorter climbs and if you are a weak climber (or out riding with quicker climbers) force yourself to the front of the group at the bottom of the climb and start at the front. As the climb progresses other riders may ease past you. By the top you may be at the back of the group or even a little way off it – but importantly you're still in contact. A little extra effort at the flatter sections of the climb will save a massive effort for several kilometres later on if you don't have to push hard to catch the group over the top of the hill.

In a race this is even more important, so consider your position in the group long before the climb begins.

Measure your effort

Consider using a power-measuring device on your bike. By knowing your maximum power output you can gauge the sort of effort you might use on the hill. You can then monitor the wattage being produced on a climb and determine what you need to produce or exceed to climb faster. Alternatively, use a stopwatch to see if you are climbing faster. Combine these figures with different gearing combinations and you have all you need to analyse your climbing.

Out of the saddle

You can get more power into the pedals by standing out of the saddle, but this is more expensive in terms of energy consumption, so it's not ideal for longer climbs. Efficiency figures vary, but climbing out of the saddle uses about 10% more energy than staying seated.

Pace yourself on long climbs and ride to a tempo you know you can maintain – you can always sprint for the summit.

Keep your hands wide on the handlebars when out of the saddle. Don't swing the bike violently from side to side – this wastes energy and may be seen as dangerous riding by race commissaries – but a gentle movement to the left as you bring your right foot down and vice versa can help your rhythm.

On some climbs you will have no choice but to get out of the saddle, either to overcome a change in gradient or perhaps to ease aching muscles. Often when riders do this they tend to 'kick back' (which can present problems if others are following closely on your back wheel) and lose some pace. Make sure you keep pressure on the pedals as you rise out of the saddle and change up a gear to maintain your speed, as you can use your weight more and invariably your cadence slows when out of the saddle. When you sit down again, you can then change down a gear to maintain cadence.

DIFFERENT DISCIPLINES

CROSS COUNTRY MOUNTAIN BIKING

Climbing is the key to success in cross country mountain bike racing. Many world-class riders have trouble with their descending but they can all climb well. If you have an edge over your opponents in climbing, you can put minutes between you and them to effectively kill off the race. Indeed, many mountain bikers have gone on to excel in the mountains of the Grand Tours – Michel Rassmussen, Cadel Evans and Santiago Botero have all swapped to the Alpine switchbacks with devastating results.

CYCLO-CROSS

Cyclo-cross climbs are unique in that they usually require the rider to dismount and start running. However, practice can result in being able to ride the most technical climbs and all but the most vertical of ascents.

AUDAX

Conservative climbing is the key to success in Audax and sportive rides. Seated, steady climbing is the best approach as it conserves energy and places less stress on the legs.

TIME TRIAL

If you can't climb fast in a time trial then you will lose a lot of time. Most time trials involve climbing at some point – even the flattest course with the slightest gradient requires careful planning and gear selection so as not to lose time. It's different to a road climb where other riders may be forcing the pace, as you are trying to maintain a constant effort and not overcook it. Use a gear that will match your cadence (try this in training). Better still, use a power meter so that you can ensure a constant effort.

Cross country mountain biking.

Cyclo-cross.

Descending

Everyone knows that climbs can show up the differences between fit and not-so-fit riders, but it's surprising how big a difference good descending makes. Some riders descend like motorcyclists (if you watch the Tour de France, it's common to see the top riders dropping the motorcycle cameramen on the big mountain descents) whereas others can be almost slower than their climbing speed. Of course, there is an element of self-preservation here, and that should be respected. It's far better to descend conservatively, within your limits, than to descend like a demon and have an accident.

Reading the terrain

Reading the road or trail ahead is vital for good descending. On the road there are plenty of clues as to which way the road twists or turns – signposts, chevrons and barriers can all indicate bends of varying degrees and will help you to anticipate how fast you can tackle a descent. You can also watch traffic ahead, noting when motorists apply their brakes to indicate sharp bends or a steeper gradient.

A professional road rider may reach speeds of a 100 kph (62.5 mph) on long descents – which takes skill and nerve.

Off-road, clues are less obvious, but nevertheless it's worth looking for them. In races you'll be able to see the course tapes, but is there a fence, wall or hedge that shows the line of the path to help you pick your line? Can you spot the tracks of other riders who have passed ahead of you? When racing, if you see a cluster or a crowd of spectators, you can be sure that there's some sort of obstacle which looks impressive as riders clear it – or not. Look out for the body language of riders ahead. If you see them sit up, move their pedals, lean to one side or stick a knee out, you can guarantee that they are slowing down, and you'll probably need to do the same.

Top speed

If your route is straight and clear, you can shift into top gear and descend at speed. Stay relaxed and concentrate on a point as far in the distance as you can.

Flick the chain onto the big chainring. This will stop it bouncing around, slapping on your chainstay or even coming off the chainring, and will bring you into a bigger gear ready for pedalling at the foot of the hill. On long or fast descents, you may prefer to freewheel. Let your legs roll over gently. You'll need to lift your inside pedal and press down on the outside pedal for any corners or bends. Rolling the cranks gently stops your legs from stiffening up on long descents and helps to ensure the chain stays in place.

A rider needs a balanced and comfortable position – arms bent and head up looking down the road.

When time trialling, you should be aiming to keep the pressure on the pedals all the time. Chris Boardman was renowned for being an expert at this. Often, club cyclists would say they had been caught by Boardman, who never seemed to get very far ahead on a climb, but once over the top of any hill he disappeared like a bullet. For him, descents weren't opportunities for a rest, but places to take advantage of gravity. By maintaining his effort on the descents – and his aerodynamic position – he could stretch his advantage over his rivals.

Position on the bike

Whatever the terrain, on-road or off-road, keep your head up, looking ahead as far as possible, sit back on the saddle and, unless you are descending on aero bars on a straight section of road, hold the widest points of handlebars within reach of the brakes. Keep a firm grip of the handlebars but relax your arms, and hold the pedals level, so that your arms and legs can act as suspension over any rough ground.

For greater speed, bend your elbows more and crouch low to bring your chin close to the handlebar stem. Keep your elbows close to your sides and bring your knees next to the top tube. If you need to brake, sit up to catch a bit more of the wind and use your body to help you slow down.

Experienced time triallists might be able to tackle almost any descent on the aero bars, but if you have any inkling that you might need to use your brakes, it's worth forgoing the aero bars and covering the brakes instead. You can still get a pretty aero position by crouching low over the handlebars – look at pictures of time triallists in the 1970s like Alf Engers and Derek Cottington and you'll see that by bending their elbows to bring their forearms almost parallel with the ground their backs are as flat, if not flatter, as anyone today using aero bars.

Mountain bikers often lean over the back wheel behind the saddle when descending.

SPEED WOBBLE

From time to time riders experience problems of 'speed wobble' when descending. There doesn't seem to be any definitive reason for this. Invariably, discussions range around the bike's geometry headset adjustment and weight distribution. This may be a small contributory factor (steep head angles, poorly adjusted headset and either too much or too little weight on the front wheel) but far more likely is the rider tensing up. In normal circumstances you make constant, small, relaxed movements to keep the bike upright. If you are tense, you find yourself fighting to counteract these movements. The more tense you are, the less stable the bike feels.

If ever you find your bike wobbling at speed downhill, relax. Take a deep breath, whistle a tune, wiggle your fingers, relax your shoulders and sit up to slow down a little – anything to overcome your tense feeling. If you need to, apply the brakes very gently, with a bit more power to the rear. Avoid looking at your handlebar computer – you can always check your maximum speed once you've reached the bottom of the hill.

Sprinting

As we saw in the skills matrix, with the exception of time trialling and cyclo-sportive rides sprinting is a vital skill to most cycling disciplines. Sprinting has to be explosive. If it's not, then it's just 'going faster'. If you are at the end of a race with anyone else, you need to outsprint them if you're going to beat them. The sprint is comprised of two elements: the jump and sustaining the speed. It has to be a 100% effort.

Technique

The keys to a good sprint are positioning and the initial acceleration or explosiveness. You can break the technique into a number of components:

- hold the handlebars firmly, and as low and wide as possible
- keep your head up, looking to where you are going
- select a large gear that you can 'get on top of' quickly
- don't begin your sprint at the front of the group – being fourth or fifth rider is usually a good position
- pull up on the handlebars
- push down hard and fast with your foot as the pedal just passes 'top dead centre'

- follow through with the other foot and increase to your maximum cadence as quickly as possible
- keep your shoulders still but allow the bike to sway slightly (not excessively) from side to side to help the pedalling action
- be prepared to 'kick' more than once if others can match your pace
- practise sprints of different lengths and starting with either foot.

Timing is everything in sprinting. Time your effort so that you are still at top speed before the finish line. If you haven't yet reached top speed, you've left it too late (or you lack 'explosiveness'). If you fade before the line, you went too early and others will pass you.

Training
Sprinting predisposes those riders with a greater proportion of fast-twitch muscle fibres (see *Pedalling*, above). Not everyone may be blessed with a naturally high proportion of these fibres but it is still possible to improve sprinting abilities with appropriate training.

Incorporate sprint training into your programme at least once a week (but don't forgo other aspects of your training or you'll not be in good enough shape to reach the finish and be in contention) – we will cover this in more detail in *Chapter 5*.

For training, use a low gear – for example 39tx17t or 18t – and sprint out of the saddle for 6–8 seconds (100–150m) and continue in the saddle for another 6 seconds (100m). Repeat this three or four times, allowing yourself a recovery time between each effort – this is one exercise where you do not want a build-up of lactic acid.

If you have the opportunity to train behind a Derny on a track (see page 40), practise coming off its wheel and sprinting past. Alternatively, you can do this with club-mates. Have them wind up the pace and practise coming past them from two or three riders back.

You also need to improve your strength and practise using your race gear. On a stretch of road or track similar to a race finish, select your finish line and begin to 'wind up' the gear to reach maximum speed with 250–300 metres to go to simulate a bunch riding into the finish. Repeat this 6–10 times.

Choose some uphill sprints (many race finishes are uphill) and some downhill. The uphill ones will help develop strength and the downhill ones will help improve your speed.

Sprinters also need upper body strength and core stability. This is where you will need to get off your bike for sessions in the gym, weight training and cross training (rowing machines are great for improving strength in these areas).

Tactics – track
Sprinting is regarded as the 'benchmark' skill for good track riders. Having a quick turn of speed can make a big difference in any track event, from 'power' events like

Road riders need to be able to sprint and then recover to sprint again – it's an important skill.

Sprinting is also a vital skill for off-road riders.

Keirin or 1km time trial (which is very much an extended sprint) to the endurance events like points races or Madisons (which have their fair share of breaking away, bridging and out and out sprinting for points or sprint laps). Whatever your preference if you want to be a track rider, sprinting is going to play a large part in your training schedule.

Tactics – on-road

Road sprinting is slightly different from track sprinting, in that the conditions (weather and road) can play a major part in the outcome. Although the techniques are very similar, not all track sprinters make good 'roadman-sprinters', as they are known. A tough uphill sprint finish will require different riding technique from a wind-assisted flat finish.

In a road race a sprint is needed for breaking away, bridging and 'getting back on' after a hill or sharp corner. All these situations require the ability to sprint and recover, many times during a race. It's therefore not all about pure power – there is an element of skill needed in selecting the right gear, manoeuvring into the right position and applying just the right amount of effort, at the right time.

Tactics – off-road

It is essential to include sprinting in your off-road training plan and it will really help at key times of the race, notably (and paradoxically) at the start rather than the finish. A good start is essential in off-road racing. Practising your sprint technique can help to get you away from the grid first, allowing a clear run so you can set the pace and your own rhythm for the race. Out-of-the-saddle efforts will also help bridge gaps to other riders and climb short, sharp hills.

It's rare that you'll finish with a sprint, but if you've added this type of effort into your training you can take confidence from the knowledge that you can if you have to.

Tactics – time trialling

The starting effort of a time trial is pretty much sprinting – but don't overdo it or you'll be gasping for breath before the end of the first kilometre. If you have any energy left at the end of a time trial, you weren't trying hard enough! However, if you can force any extra pace at the end of your ride, you may gain a vital second or two – which could gain you enough advantage to move up the finishing order by a couple of places.

Group riding

When you first ride in a group you may be slightly unsure as to what is going on. Where should you be riding in the formation? Who is in charge? How does it all work?

There are a few rules to riding in a group safely and effectively. There is also some basic riding 'etiquette' you need to know, just so you don't upset anyone. The main rules of group riding are to:

· look out for one another
· ride sensibly
· consider the weaker riders.

It's not a race, so you can forget trying to beat the group back to the rendezvous – it's about racking up the miles or kilometres at a steady pace and in good company.

Why ride in a group?

There are many compelling reasons for riding in a group – social, safety, sporting and fitness benefits. Of course, if you are new to the sport or the area, you'll learn some new training routes without getting lost. You are also less likely to be bothered by other road users and they are far more likely to see you and allow for this in their

A small group will always work better than a very large one.

driving. By riding in a group you'll also learn essential road skills and be able to chat to more experienced riders. Generally speaking, riding with a group is the best place to learn about how to progress in the sport.

Find a ride suitable for your level

Once upon a time, weekend club runs were fast and furious – if you couldn't keep up they would leave you in the middle of nowhere with no food and no map. Happily, things have changed.

Cycling is now one of the easiest and most sociable sports to get into. You can easily find a club run near you, usually just by asking at your local bike shop or searching for the local club websites via the national governing bodies. However, it's best to ask if the rides are quick, or social, and how far they usually go. Best to find out beforehand – especially if you arrive at the meet to find four pro riders who will probably ride for four or five hours at over 20mph without breaking into a sweat!

Group sizing

The choice is a simple one: small group or large?

- Big group – how many riders there are usually determines how coordinated the group is and a big group is not always a better one. It will 'concertina' and become erratic, coming together and moving apart at varying speeds. This will usually result in the group fragmenting as the weaker riders can't maintain the pace and 'lose the wheel' of the rider in front of them. This is very similar to a road race peloton and trying to get 12–20 riders to ride in a group steadily and efficiently is very difficult.

- Small group – a well organised group of four to six riders of equal ability will always travel faster than a huge peloton of mixed ability riders. Riders can still ride fast and gain enough recovery in the slipstream of the others in the group before taking another turn. Riders may well miss turns if they are tiring but generally the pace will not drop until the group begins to tire or they lose more than one rider.

Group formations

There are a number of formations and roles that you will need to know about if you are to take part in as an active member in a group ride.

Ride in two lines

Two parallel lines of riders is usually the safest and most practical riding formation. Club runs and group training rides the world over will assume this formation, usually with the ride leader at the front and another experienced rider towards the back. The normal group etiquette is to maintain formation – overtaking (just because you feel fitter and quicker) is generally frowned upon. The chances are that there will be a number of riders in the group who could 'work you over' if they so wish but that's just not done on social rides.

Riding in two lines is perfectly legal and it is at the discretion of the riders to single

WIND DIRECTION

This can influence the side at which the riders move up and down. The idea is to get the most shelter prior to leading the group. If the wind is blowing from the right, this will be the line that moves back, providing shelter to the advancing riders on the left and vice versa. The result is an angled and stepped shape called an echelon, essentially like a flock of migrating birds. When this happens in a small group it is even more important to get the echelon working right. One rider will usually take charge and shout orders, so listen out for instructions when the wind changes direction or the group turns a corner.

out. However, on single lane roads and busy main roads it's often wise to ride in single file – be sensible and don't get in the way of fast-moving traffic or impatient motorists.

Changing over

From time to time, the front two riders may tire slightly and need a rest from either riding into the wind or dragging the group over a few hills – setting the pace is hard work. They may peel off the front at the same time, together (see *Figures 1* and *2*). Or they may swap over by one rider on the outside moving to the front and taking the lead, then the outside line shifting up two positions, basically changing partners all the way down the string of riders – this is known as the chaingang (see *Figure 3*). Apart from anything else if you are socialising it's a good way to keep the conversation going!

FIGURE 1 – FRONT RIDERS PEEL OFF TOGETHER TO ONE SIDE OF THE GROUP

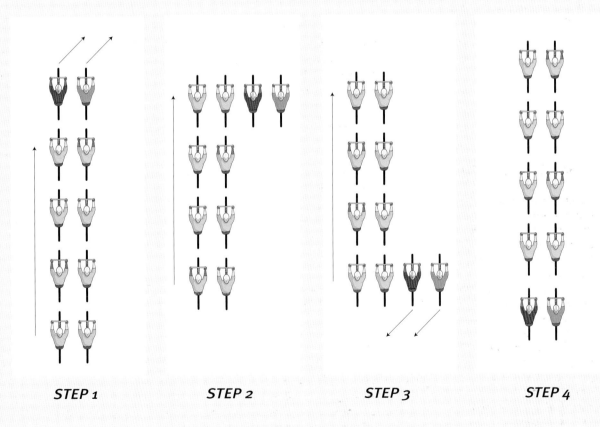

STEP 1   STEP 2   STEP 3   STEP 4

FIGURE 2 – FRONT RIDERS PEEL OFF TO OPPOSITE SIDES OF THE GROUP

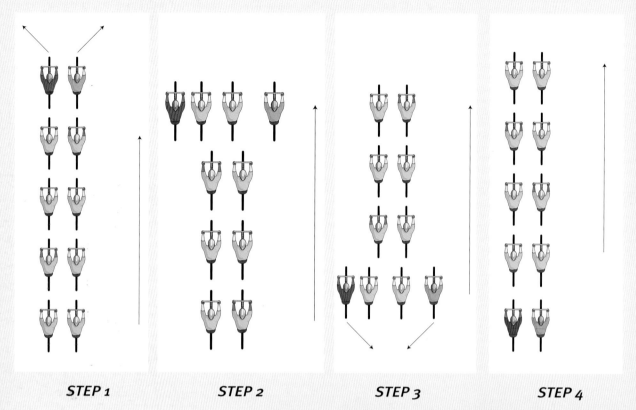

STEP 1   STEP 2   STEP 3   STEP 4

FIGURE 3 – FRONT RIDERS PEEL OFF ONE AT A TIME – THE CHAINGANG

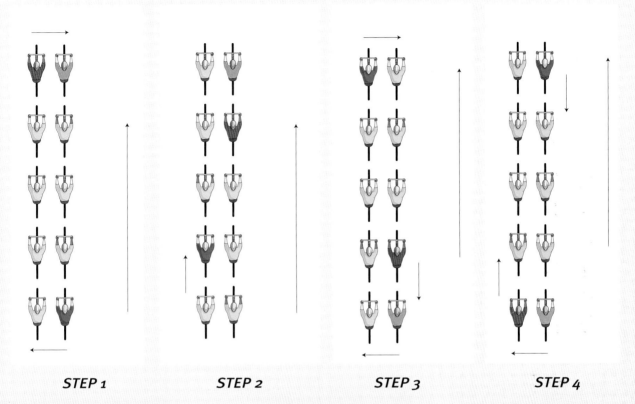

STEP 1   STEP 2   STEP 3   STEP 4

'CAR UP' OR 'CAR BACK'
A general warning of a car trying to pass or one coming around a corner. A car coming towards you is usually 'Car up' although sometimes this can be 'Oil up' depending on where you are riding.

'HEADS UP' OR 'LOOK UP'
If this is shouted it usually means there is a bad junction or potential hazard ahead and to pay attention. Ride leaders should warn you of pending problems in the road. This is especially important if you are in a large group and it will take a while to get around the hazard – but that's no excuse not to pay attention at all times.

'SINGLE OUT'
When a car is behind and needs extra space to overtake, or if the group is approaching a narrow road or overtaking a line of parked cars.

Don't be tempted to ride off the front – maintain the pace of the group at all times.

Don't ride off the front

Depending on the type of group you are riding in, the main principle of group riding is to ride together (either socially or 'through and off' – see below). Attacking off the front is not a good idea, it will usually upset the more experienced riders and generally upset the discipline and pace of the group. A disciplined group will probably just let you go to 'fry' out on your own until you tire.

Sometimes there will be a long hill or section where there will be some hard riding allowed. Often there may be a sprint for a town sign, but remember to be sensible, this isn't a race and there are riders in the group who may be dropped or start to suffer if you want to do your Zone 4 effort 30mi. from home. (See *Chapter 5* for more on training zones.)

Through and off

Sometimes known as 'swapping off' or as a 'chaingang', this type of riding is the choreographed element to group riding. It is ideal for when you want to travel a bit quicker and use all the available firepower in the group, or even just to share the workload on a social ride. Learning the ropes takes a few rides and usually there will be a slower group for you to start out in. Two lines of riders travel at different speeds. Riders shelter behind each other until it is their turn to lead. The key is to stay close the wheel in front, and not to increase the pace (half wheeling) when you're at the front. Typically, turns at the front of chaingang are short, doing just 30 pedal revolutions before moving across and back into a sheltered position is common. Use a similar gear to the other riders, ride steadily and look ahead to anticipate any problems, changes in speed or direction.

A good chaingang runs smoothly with almost telepathic communication between the riders. The ultimate example of this precision technique is the team pursuit on the track where riders change at high speed and maintain no more than centimetres off each others' wheels.

Save the power

When you reach the front of the group you should 'pull your turn' of equal time and effort to the other riders. You need to ride steadily. Going too fast on the way to front may create gaps behind you as riders struggle with the change in pace and going too slow may mean that the rider behind you comes through too fast as they try to rescue the tempo. You need to judge carefully how hard to pedal according to the agreed pace of the group. This can all change when you start racing, of course, but even so, riding steadily is an essential skill. In training, the idea is for all the riders to get a workout and to work on their bike skills, so speed is not the most important factor.

Stay close

The benefits of riding in a group are more than just social. You will cover more ground with less effort in a group, saving around 20% of your energy when sitting on a wheel in the bunch – stay close to the rider in front to maximise the slipstream and to allow riders around you to also use it to best effect. If the rider ahead appears to be unsteady, ride just a few centimetres to one side so that if he (or she) does slow suddenly, you can slide alongside them without making contact. Keep the rider in front in your near vision but look ahead, beyond them, so that you can see what's happening.

Don't 'switch' suddenly

Hold your line and keep a steady cadence. The rider behind you needs to be close to you but also needs to be confident that you won't brake suddenly or switch direction. Unless something really drastic happens, the riders in front will not stop suddenly without warning, so you won't have to make any sudden moves.

GENERAL HAND SIGNALS

HAND UP IN THE AIR
Usually signifies that the rider signalling is stopping (e.g. for a puncture) or there is a hazard in the road that the whole group may have to stop for.

POINTING OUT HOLES IN THE ROAD
Even when racing, if you have to go around something in the road you need to indicate this to the riders behind before they hit it. This is sometimes called 'spotting', and is essential in group riding situations. You must point out drain covers, holes, road kill, glass or anything which may cause harm to a cyclist.

INDICATING DIRECTIONS TO RIDERS BEHIND
Whether it is slowing down or turning at junctions, large groups need everyone to indicate for other road users, so let them know what you intend to do.

WAVING FOR PARKED CARS, HORSES AND PEDESTRIANS
When overtaking, riders will sometimes wave a hand behind them – this signifies there is a hazard that means the group will have to move out. They will do this by 'wafting' a hand behind their back in the direction that they intend to move to indicate to the riders behind. Remember you are expected to do the same so the rider behind you has seen the obstacle. Move out slowly and try to avoid swerving.

If you get 'shelled out' or fall off the pace, let the group know so that they can either send a rider back to help or wait at the next junction.

Resting riders

Keeping the pace of the group steady often means trying to stay in approximately the same gear, spinning a similar cadence. Many riders make the mistake of thinking that they should always ride in the big ring and as fast as possible. However, in the training environment you'll get much more out of the group ride if you work on your cadence and spin a little faster – this will develop your pedalling technique and improve your efficiency.

Lastly, remember that group riding is all about the group, not the individual. Many political thinkers in the peloton over the years have likened it to a socialist collaboration. We are all working for a common goal. We work for one another and everyone will pull their weight. Of course, this utopian ideal all falls down when someone decides to attack...

Tell someone if you have a problem

You may be feeling a bit shy about it at first, but tell the riders around you if you have a puncture or mechanical problem, don't drift to the back and off the pace without telling anyone. If they drop you on a hill they should wait or send a rider or two back to pace you up to the group so don't worry, they won't abandon you.

Send the message to the front

If you are riding at the back and a rider has been dropped for whatever reason, tell the riders in front of you and ask them to shout up to the front, so that the leaders know to slow the pace to suit the problem or the group can stop. Once riders have been left behind, finding them and regrouping can be difficult.

Stopping for a break

Traditionally, a club run will make a café stop. This usually happens about halfway around the ride or sometimes (and probably more sensibly) you will stop at the end of the ride or near to the original rendezvous point – this way you can still have a chat and get cold without having to ride for another three hours before you get home!

Theories on this are mixed – coaches mainly have a dim view on breaking halfway through a long ride (after all, it's only cricket that stops for tea and cake in the middle of a competition). After ten minutes or so, your body goes into recovery mode and getting back on the bike can be very hard indeed. However, it can be argued that by breaking a ride into two parts, it can executed at greater intensity and, especially after the racing season, it can provide essential R&R for the racing cyclist and allow them to catch up with the local riding gossip.

In short, we'd say wait for the end of the ride for a café stop and avoid the cakes!

Other useful skills

It sounds simple but a few riders lack the skills to take a drink or even signal effectively when riding. Stretching and changing your clothing are more advanced techniques but if you haven't practised them you may have problems should you ever compete at higher levels.

Drinking

Taking a drink on the move is fundamental to your success as a bike rider. You can't pull over to the side of the road to get your bottle and swig your drink. Everyone will leave you behind and you'll waste loads of time coming to a halt and getting back up to speed.

Follow a few key points and you will be fine:
- Look where you are going at all times
- Hold your handlebars either on the brake hoods or tops of the bars if you have dropped handlebars
- Practise reaching down to remove and replace your bottle in its cage without having to look at it. You may need to turn your knee out, or freewheel a little, to keep your leg out of the way, but try not to lose speed
- If you're riding in a group, take a drink when you're at the back of the line rather than when in the middle or on the front
- Hold the bottle to one side and with the nozzle in your mouth, tilt the bottle up and squeeze it rather than tilting your head back. (The same technique applies when time trialling, but you may prefer to get off your aerobars to be more stable when drinking.)

Drinking on the move is a key skill – pro riders, like Jan Ullrich, can even manage it while descending.

On-the-bike stretches are well worth doing, but be sure to stay in control of the bike.

- Take a drink before you are about to overtake a rider. This will lend you a bit of mystery if no one ever sees you drink on your ride!
- If you have helpers at the roadside for a time trial, have them hold your bottle by its neck with their fingertips, up at shoulder height and run in the same direction as you. You'll need to drop your original bottle on the road-side close to their feet and reach out to collect your bottle from them. As you grip the bottle, they let go.

In road race feeds, helpers need to stand still, facing the riders with a bottle held for the riders to collect in a similar fashion. Helpers are best located where riders aren't travelling too fast – on slight uphill drags or near the top of a hill are best.

Mountain bikers often prefer Camelbak or Platypus drinking systems – a small ruck-sack with an internal bladder and drinking tube. This makes drinking on the move much easier. The drinking tube has a 'bite valve' so once the rider has it in his mouth he can draw drink without taking his hands from the handlebars. The tube will have a Velcro wrap so it can be secured on the rucksack chest strap when not being used.

You need to anticipate your fluid needs and drink before the toughest parts of a ride. Drink before you get to the steep hills, or where you lose least time.

Changing clothing

You need to be confident about riding 'no hands' before you attempt to pull on a gilet or remove a long-sleeve jersey over your helmet. Full-zip jackets or jerseys are easi-er to deal with than shorter-zipped garments but make sure you can get the cuffs over your gloves. Bear in mind that you normally put on your gloves or track mitts after your jersey so they probably need to come off before you try to take off your jer-sey or racing cape. Practise putting garments on and taking them off when riding your turbo trainer. Be very careful not to let the garment catch in the wheels or on the handlebars – that's a sure way of crashing.

On the road, you'll also have to contend with the wind, speed, proximity to other rid-ers and traffic – as well as your balance. Use the wind direction to your advantage to help billow out the garment and make it easier to slip your arms in or out of it. And what are you going to do with garments you do discard? Will they scrunch up small enough to fit in your pockets along with your bonk rations and whatever else you're carrying? If there's the slightest hint that you are not comfortable changing your clothes on the move, don't do it. You'll just have to suffer with what you've got on until you can stop and change.

Stretching

On a long ride or even in a race you may feel tight or aching muscles. Rather than stop at the side of the road for some stretching exercises, you can stretch on the bike. Unless the group you're riding with is travelling very slowly, it's best if you move to the back of the group. At least if you do lose your balance you won't affect anyone else. It's a simple matter to sit up, no-handed, and stretch your back or shoulders while still pedalling. You'll have to freewheel to stretch your calf muscles: keep your hands on the brake levers and drop one heel below the pedal. Hold it for a few seconds and repeat with the other leg. Similarly, you can unclip your foot to grab your ankle and pull back to stretch your quadriceps – but make sure you don't kick your back wheel as you do this.

Components of Fitness

Introduction

What do we mean by the words 'fit' or 'fitness'? Having the fitness to compete in a cycling road race is not the same as being fit to run a marathon or play a game of squash. There are very different demands on the body for all these sporting activities. Have a look at the next parade of Olympic athletes and you'll see a whole spectrum of body sizes and shapes represented. They're all supremely fit, but the rower's fitness and physique is very different from that of the dance gymnast and the cycling track sprinters who, in turn, have quite obvious build and fitness differences to the road and endurance riders.

By fitness we mean 'fitness for purpose' or, put simply, fitness to do the particular job or sport that we want to excel at. In this sense, fitness is a combination of strength, speed and stamina coupled with flexibility and mental toughness. All sporting activities have varying combinations of these ingredients. Each one of us is better predisposed to some of these elements than others, but with training and exercise – in varying degrees of duration, frequency and intensity – we can influence and improve all of the components of fitness.

This chapter will enable you to identify your own fitness strengths and goals and, combined with the skills matrix in *Chapter 2*, will help you to either identify your strongest cycling disciplines or help you to focus on developing specific areas of your fitness to perform best in the discipline of your choice. It also gives you a basic overview of the components of fitness and training which you will need in order to make the most of the training plans in *Chapter 5*. It is by no means a definitive guide to general fitness – countless books could, and have, been written on this subject.

Fitness Matrix

Much like the skills matrix in *Chapter 2*, the fitness matrix will enable you to map your fitness to the various cycling disciplines, each of which has a unique blend of required fitness components that you will need in order to take part and compete.

The matrix lists the various fitness elements and refers them to each cycling discipline – each element is then given a rating of 1–5 depending on how important it is to the discipline in question. For example, aerobic endurance is crucial for road racing (and therefore gets a rating of 5) but is of far less benefit to the downhill mountain biker (and therefore gets a rating of 1).

FITNESS MATRIX

	ROAD RACING	TIME TRIAL 10–25 MILES	TIME TRIAL 50–100 MILES	TIME TRIAL 12–24 HOURS	TRACK SPRINT	TRACK ENDU-RANCE	MOUNTAIN BIKE XC	MOUNTAIN BIKE DOWN-HILL	CYCLO-CROSS	CYCLO-SPORTIVE
AEROBIC ENDURANCE	5	4	4	5	1	3	5	1	4	5
MUSCULAR SPEED	5	3	3	3	5	4	4	4	4	2
STRENGTH	4	4	3	2	5	4	4	5	4	2
MUSCLE POWER	4	3	3	2	5	4	4	5	4	1
SHORTTERM MUSCLE ENDURANCE	3	2	1	1	5	4	3	4	3	1
FLEXIBILITY	3	3	4	5	3	4	5	5	5	2

Aerobic endurance (stamina)

This is the ability to maintain a continuous activity – at a fairly low intensity – for an extended period of time. With the vast majority of cycling events lasting more than 60 seconds, aerobic endurance is a key component of almost any cyclist's fitness.

With training, the rider develops:
- improved cardio-respiratory and muscle systems with a bigger, stronger heart that can transport more oxygen-rich blood per heart beat
- an increase in the number of red blood cells which allows more oxygen to be transported to the muscles
- stronger and more efficient breathing and lung capacity
- an increase in the glycogen stored in the muscles
- improved ability to produce energy.

Improved technique also allows a rider use energy more efficiently.

Muscular speed (cadence)

In physiological terms, speed is the rate of muscle movement. In cycling terms, this equates to cadence – the rate of pedalling, measured in revolutions per minute (rpm) (see *Chapter 2*) – not the velocity of a rider. Ideal pedalling speeds depend on the terrain and circumstances but are generally in the 80–100rpm range. Top track sprinters have been measured with peak cadences of 250rpm on ergometers and are in the region of 160–180rpm in competition.

Cadence can be improved by using low gears, training with a tailwind or downhill. Developing a high cadence (over 90rpm) by training helps to:
- increase the efficiency of the neural pathways and energy systems
- improve pedalling technique and the ability to change pace
- maintain high cadences
- improve maximum cadence.

Strength

The maximum amount of force that a muscle or group of muscles can exert against a resistance is 'strength'. Increasing the load on the muscle or group of muscles will result in improved strength (think of weight training). Using a bigger gear at the same cadence or riding in hilly territory instead of flat lands will result in improved strength. It helps riders to be stronger so that they can turn bigger gears or maintain a good stance on the bike when climbing or descending (particularly off-road).

Muscle Power (speed x strength)

Any improvement in either strength or speed of muscle movement will create improved muscle power – the ability to produce a very high power output over a very short period of time (about 20 seconds). Muscle power is required for sudden, fast movements or increases in pace to overcome resistance, such as standing start, or commencing sprint efforts. Top time-triallists typically produce maximum muscle power values of around 830 watts, compared to around 1,100 watts for road and cross-country mountain-bike riders and 1,350 watts for track riders.

Aerobic endurance and muscular speed are the key requirements for the road racer.

Improved muscular power results in:
- more groups of muscle fibres be recruited for faster and more efficient muscle contraction
- neural pathways from the brain to the muscles becoming more efficient
- as the muscles increase in size and strength, the rider being able to exert more force on the pedals
- the ability to hold the bike more upright (particularly important for off-road riding)
- being able to maintain an appropriate body position (such as a low, aero-dynamic profile for pursuit riding on the track or time-trialling on the road).

Short-term muscular endurance

This is the ability to sustain high power over a limited period of time. The intensity of the effort is such that it cannot be maintained for long (roughly 20 seconds to about 20 minutes maximum) without significant fatigue.

Improved short-term muscular endurance results in:
- improved neural pathway efficiency
- better use of short-term energy stores
- better expulsion of waste from the muscles for delayed or reduced onset of fatigue
- better recovery after high intensity efforts.

Flexibility

Flexibility is the range of movement at a joint or series of joints and is needed to:
- swing a leg over the saddle to mount the bike
- look behind to check traffic
- maintain a low, aerodynamic position for time-trialling
- twist the upper body for Madison riding on the track or take a feed on the move in a long-distance event
- move around the bike for balance in mountain bike or cyclo-cross events.

Flexibility can be improved by stretching exercises – although stretching is very indi-vidual and it should not be done competitively. Being able to stretch or reach further than another rider will not necessarily make you faster. However, if you can achieve a lower time-trial position than a similarly powered rival, you will present a lower profile to the wind and travel faster for the same power output. Having a greater range of movement can also help to reduce injuries. If you fall, twist or have to hold an extreme position, the greater range of movement will provide a buffer zone before your joints are flexed beyond their capacity and injury occurs.

Stretching

Cyclists are not known for their flexibility. In sporting terms we're probably as far away from ballet dancers as you can get. Nevertheless, stretching is an essential part of injury prevention and recovery 'strategy'. It is also relaxing, promotes circu-lation and increases a range of motion, which is good for you whatever you do.

Many coaches have their favourite stretches and riders often develop their own routines to suit their particular needs. Some of the stretches here will work for you, some may not – it's a case of try them and see.

When stretching, ensure that the muscles are warm – for example get on the bike for 10–15 minutes of gentle pedalling. And never 'bounce' – be sure to keep the movement fluid. You should stretch after competition or training. In addition, try to incorporate stretching into your daily exercise routine – try to put aside 10–20 minutes to go through your routine at whatever times fits best with your schedule.

Hamstrings

This is the usual hamstring stretch and the usual bad way to do it. The spine is bent and the pivot for the stretch is not coming from the hips, plus you are putting all your upper body weight on your lower spine. Instead, flatten your back and place the arms out in front of you onto a rail or similar static object, then you can keep the back straight and slowly stretch the hamstrings. Hold for 30 seconds each time.

An easier – and safer – way to stretch the hamstrings is to sit flat like this and bend forward from the hips, reaching down the leg toward your foot to help support the body. Again, try to keep the back as flat as possible and bend at the hips – feel the stretch gently, hold for anything up to a minute then slowly release and swap legs. Feel the stretch in the rear of the upper part of the leg, especially behind the knee. Repeat a few times during a routine.

Quads

Cyclists find the quadriceps stretch a bit difficult not to do, but to get enough stretch into the muscle. Simply standing upright and pulling the foot towards your bottom isn't always the best way. To get a bigger stretch sit on your feet and support your body weight with your hands, allowing a little stretch by carefully leaning backwards. Keep the back straight. Be careful with this stretch if you have knee issues as it can be painful, also don't do it on hard ground either as your bony knees will really hurt after a short while. Feel the stretch in the front of the quad. Hold for 15–20 seconds and repeat.

Calves

The calf muscles can get incredibly tight when cycling and this stretch is excellent for releasing the tired muscle. It looks a bit like you are trying to push a wall over and although it shouldn't be that hard this is what you are trying to simulate, albeit with one leg locked out and pivoting on it's ankle to stretch the calf. Feel the stretch behind the knee and down the calf. You can place the stretched leg further from the wall for an increased stretch. Do 30 seconds on each leg and repeat several times over during the routine.

Abductors

Stretching the groin area is usually something neglected by cyclists and yet it's a very important area for firing and supporting the larger muscle groups in the tops of the legs. Sit upright and draw your feet towards your groin until you can feel a stretch. Then grab your ankles and brace your elbows against the knees, force the knees towards the ground and stretch the groin 'manually'. Hold for 20–30 seconds and repeat.

Glutes and lower back

This twist stretches the back and hip area and is effective for releasing tension from the lower back. Bend one leg and place the foot of this leg over by the side of the opposite knee. Then trap the knee of the bent leg with the elbow of the opposite arm. Place the other arm directly behind your body and then turn your hips to allow you to see directly behind you . . . it sounds like a game of Twister but it's highly effective.

Lower back and hip flexors

This cross-legged stretch is for the lower back and hip flexors. Lie flat on the ground and bend one leg. Then place the opposite ankle on top of the bent knee. Clasp your hands behind your upper leg and pull both legs towards your chest. You will feel the stretch in the hips and gluteus regions of the crossed over leg. Hold for 20 seconds and change legs.

Lower back

This simple stretch works wonders for the lower back and can be done whilst watching the TV. Simply curl up in a ball and pull the knees towards your chest. Just a small stretch each time and you'll feel it in the gluteus, mid and lower back muscles. Hold for 30 seconds and release slowly. Repeat.

Neck

Here the rider is showing a stretch to help loosen the neck muscles. It's a resistance type exercise where the head is pressing against the hand and holding the muscles in tension, for 20 seconds and then slowly releasing. It's also a good one to do when sitting in front of a computer for hours on end typing!

Also clasp the hands together and reach above your head and towards the ceiling and hold for 25 seconds – this stretches out the shoulders and the arms.

Arms

Stretching the arms should also be done to relieve the tension in the shoulder and neck, especially after long days in the saddle. Bend your elbow as if to scratch the opposite ear, behind your head. Then with the other hand grasp the elbow of the bent arm and pull it firmly but steadily toward it. You will feel the stretch all down the triceps and shoulder muscles on the bent arm side. Hold for 20 seconds and repeat.

The systems of the body

Broadly speaking, there are seven systems or components of the physical body. These are:

- the skeletal system
- joints
- cartilage, tendons and ligaments
- muscular system
- energy systems
- heart and circulation
- respiratory system.

As we have said, it would be easy to write a whole book on this subject, or indeed on each one of these components, so we do not propose to look at every system here. But it is worth taking a brief look at two of them.

Muscular system

As cyclists, we are primarily concerned with skeletal muscle (as opposed to cardiac muscle or smooth muscle, which looks after our digestive system among other things) – after all it accounts for about 40% of our body weight and is the only muscle that we can control.

Skeletal muscle fibres are broadly grouped into two types known as fast and slow twitch. The 'twitch' relates to the speed of contraction of a single electrical impulse from the brain – both twitches are very quick, it's just that the slow fibres are slow relative to the fast ones.

Slow-twitch fibres (also known as type 1 or red fibres) are used in endurance activities and posture control. This is because the fibres contract smoothly and do not generate as much force as fast-twitch fibres, but they are more resistant to fatigue. They use oxygen and fat as their main source of fuel.

Fast-twitch fibres (also known as type 2 or white fibres) are used for explosive force, but are quick to fatigue. These fibres can be further divided into two types:

- type 2a fibres produce more force than type 1 but not as much as type 2b. These fibres are brought into use when type 1 fibres cannot cope with the workload of an exercise.
- type 2b fibres are the most forceful fibres and are recruited when both type 1 and type 2a fibres cannot cope with the workload. They are solely anaerobic and therefore are quick to fatigue.

The combination of these fibres is largely a matter of genetics. Therefore, our propensity to excel at sprinting or endurance events is principally determined by our parents! However, with appropriate training it is possible to recruit more of each fibre and improve their capacity to work. There is some recent research to suggest that we also have some fibres which may sit in between these two types, ready to be trained as necessary.

Fast-, or slow-twitch? Your muscle type will define your riding.

The 'average man' has 40–50% slow twitch fibres and 50–60% fast-twitch fibres. For trained cyclists, the figures are rather different, depending on their forte, as the table below shows.

MUSCLE FIBRE PERCENTAGES BY EVENT

EVENT AND APPROX DURATION	% SLOW-TWITCH FIBRE	% FAST-TWITCH FIBRE
SPRINTERS 1,000M (OVER 1 MINUTE)	25	75
CRITERIUM (OVER 1 HOUR)	50	50
50 MILE (80KM) TT (1HOUR 55 MINUTES)	75	25
200KM ROAD RACE (4HOURS 20 MINUTES)	60	40

Adapted from 'Inside the Cyclist, Physiology for the two-wheeled athlete.' Burke, Perez and Hodges, Velo-news Corporation, Revised edition 1986.

THE TRAINING EFFECT

To improve as a cyclist you need to ride a bike longer or harder, or do specific off-the-bike training. As you exercise your muscles actually get damaged. If you continue training for a long time your muscles may become so damaged that you will be literally worn out and unable to carry on. With more intense activities (racing at speed, frequent climbing or sprinting) the fatigue may be induced by a build-up of lactic acid in the muscles (see *Energy systems*, below) and pain will stop you.

Remarkably, the human body is capable of self-repair. Muscles damaged by exercise in training or racing rebuild when you are asleep (and aided by appropriate protein nutrition). But better than that, your muscles get repaired to a higher specification in order to cope with the demands just experienced. The key to improved fitness lies in balancing the amount of exertion (intensity and duration) and the amount of rest (frequency of exercise) in order to maximise the beneficial training effect. If the activity is too intense, more muscle damage will occur and your body will need more time to effect repairs. If another training session begins before you have properly recovered and rebuilt the muscle tissue to the improved specification this will exacerbate the muscle damage and lead to excessive fatigue.

You must also bear in mind the dangers of undertraining. Remember that your body wants to be 'fit for purpose' and will not carry muscle if it is not being used. If you leave long intervals between training sessions your body will not keep the improved muscles, but will let them atrophy, leaving you weaker for your next ride (see *Reversibility*, below).

You will reap the rewards of improved performance from hard training and racing.

Energy systems

In sports terms, anything lasting much beyond 60 seconds is deemed an endurance activity. This places nearly all cycling disciplines as endurance events – the main exceptions being the team sprint and match sprint events, and women's 500m time trial. At just over 60 seconds, the men's 1,000m time trial is on the cusp of sprint and endurance.

There are three main energy systems that are responsible for supplying muscles with the ATP energy that they require to function:

- ATP-CP (creatine phosphate system)
- Anaerobic (lactic acid)
- Aerobic (glucose or fat).

These systems work together and the body draws upon each according to the type of effort, its duration and the type of muscle fibre being used.

Each energy source is defined by a capacity (the total amount of potential energy, measured in kilojoules, kJ) and a power (the amount of energy usable within a unit of time, measured in watts, W). As an analogy, compare this to a barrel of water, where the capacity is the barrel's volume and the power is the flow from the tap.

ATP-CP system

The body's ATP stores last for about 4 seconds before they need to be topped up (or re-synthesised). The ATP-CP system can do this very quickly but it only has a limited supply – it can be used for about 10 seconds, but can be used again and again as long as a recovery period of about three minutes is allowed.

This system is used to fire the body into action – think of it as a first gear in a car, it gets you started but in order to run the car (your body) efficiently you will quickly need to shift into second gear (a different energy system).

Anaerobic energy system

The anaerobic ('without oxygen') energy system is used at the start of exercise when there is not enough oxygen in the muscles so glucose has to be broken down without oxygen. This system is used for short efforts, sprinting or hill-climbing but cannot be maintained for much over 60 seconds. After this time, the system starts to produce lactic acid which builds up and eventually inhibits muscle contraction.

In downhill mountain biking the fitness emphasis is on strength and muscle power.

A reduction in effort allows the lactic acid to dissipate and exercise to continue. Fast-twitch muscles use this form of energy. Lactic acid begins to build up at 60–70% of the muscle's maximum capacity, increasing in direct proportion to work. At very high levels of work, the production of lactic acid is constant. That's when the effort really hurts. Top sprinters can produce over 2,000W but the energy is used very quickly and it takes 6–8 minutes recovery after a maximal effort.

Keeping with the car analogy, think of this system as second gear.

Aerobic energy system

The aerobic ('with oxygen') energy system kicks in after a few minutes of exercise. This system uses oxygen along with either glucose or fat. As long as the intensity is not too high and there is oxygen present there will be no build up of lactic acid. This is the system most used by cyclists of all disciplines. It fuels the slow-twitch muscle fibres which are full of enzymes vital to aerobic energy supply.

The body can store enough glycogen to fuel this system for about 2–3 hours (your training will have an impact on this time). If you do not keep glycogen levels topped up then this system will lose efficiency and will be forced to burn body fat. This may sound like a good thing, but it is hard on the body – far better to keep your glucose levels topped up with regular refuelling.

Typically aerobic power is in the region of 300–400W for most racing, but sprinting demands may be around 1,500–1,700W. Think of this as the cruising gear for your car – long, sustained driving at a steady pace.

Components of training

We will look at the specifics of training in *Chapter 5*, but it is worth familiarising yourself with the basics that will determine how a training programme is put together and why it must be specific to the individual.

There are a number of factors which determine the effectiveness of training:
- specificity and fitness for purpose
- individual differences
- periodisation
- adaptation
- progression
- variation
- overload
- over-training, rest and recovery
- reversability.

Aerobic endurance and flexibility top the fitness list for triallists.

Specificity and fitness for purpose

To ride a bicycle efficiently you need to develop specific muscles to power the pedals and have the cardiovascular plumbing to cope with your body's oxygen needs. You cannot expect to be a good cyclist without riding a bike. You need to get conditioned to sitting on a saddle and to develop the skills to handle a bike and improve your riding technique. The vast majority of your training time needs to be spent on a bicycle, developing particular muscle movements and strength. This is 'specificity' and it applies to any sport.

This point is fundamental to your training and underpins the fitness matrix at the beginning of this chapter. For any type of event, you need to match your training to these components. If you are keen to ride cyclo-sportive events, there is little point in spending your time sprint training (short-term muscular endurance) when the main component of fitness is, by far, aerobic endurance. Of course, the converse is true of those who fancy their chances as match sprinters or kilometre champions.

Individual differences

Whatever training you do, there is no guarantee that you'll be better than the next rider. We all have our own genetic make-up and situation. Age, gender, level of fitness, nutrition and genes all affect our motivation and ability to adapt to training and athletic performance. Some riders like the cut and thrust of bunch racing, others prefer the individual nature of time trials. Some perform well in the heat when others wilt in the same conditions. Some relish adverse conditions and others switch off mentally, unable to motivate themselves to race in poor weather.

Riders react differently to training also. Depending on their muscle fibre composition, some will make bigger gains in speed training sessions. Other riders may have difficulty in dealing with a change of pace, but have excellent stamina and might be extremely good at time-trialling or revel in cyclo-sportive and mountain bike enduro events.

Luckily, cycling is a wide enough sport for everyone, whatever their ability, to find at least one or two areas for them to excel and gain great enjoyment from it.

The age-old question

Since cycling is a weight-bearing activity, riders can be competitive long after athletes in other sports have hung up their equipment or been forced to stop through a career of injuries. As you age beyond about 30 years, fast-twitch fibres decline more rapidly than slow-twitch ones, resulting in a gradual loss of some of your sprinting ability and top-end speed. Look at the results of the Masters World Track Championships and with few exceptions you can plot an almost straight-line correlation of increasing age against decreasing speed for events like the sprint and pursuit.

The good news is that longer races often favour the older riders as these are usually run off at a more consistent pace and shrewd riders can use their years of experience to pay dividends as they can read races better to position themselves and conserve their energy until the crucial moments. This is one contributory reason why time trials, particularly those at 80km (50 mi.) or over, cyclo-sportive and mountain-bike enduro events are dominated by older riders.

Cyclo-sportive riding is all about endurance...

Over about 40 years old riders invariably find their ability to recover suffers after intensive training sessions or hard races. This makes it very difficult for most veterans to be competitive at stage races or championships held over a number of days. With age overtaking ability, older riders may need to train harder to remain on terms with riders half their age, and still allow themselves more recovery time.

Periodisation

Not really a component of training, more an approach to it, but periodisation has become the basis of most coaches' training programmes so it is worth acquainting yourself with the basics.

The periodisation approach to training organises time into three different periods, fitting specific aims into each unit.

- *Macro-cycles* – this is usually a complete 'season' or year, although it could be 4 or 5 years covering the period from one Olympic event to the next.
- *Meso-cycles* – this cycle usually lasts 2–6 weeks and forms the building blocks of training and competition. For competitive cyclists, these blocks are: foundation or preparation, pre-competition or transition phase, competition and recovery.
- *Micro-cycles* – these subdivide the meso-cycle into small units, usually 7–14 days. Each cycle will have a specific goal or aim to hone a single skill or fitness component. It may also cover a tapering process prior to a big event to ensure that a rider is adequately rested and not fatigued prior to competition or a major target of the season.

...whereas cross country mountain biking also requires flexibility and power.

The year planner below indicates how you might divide your year (macro-cycle) if you were aiming to peak for a major race or other event in early July, like the Etape du Tour. There is a build-up to an event (maybe a stage race or long randonnée) at the end of May, followed by a brief recovery period and then a second build-up toward the main goal at the end of the second meso-cycle.

By dividing the periods into manageable meso-cycles, you can aim to bring yourself to peak condition at the end of each period. The end of each period (or beginning of the subsequent period) is a good opportunity for a brief rest to help you to recuperate fully before embarking on the next phase approaching your goal. The micro-cycles are not covered in the plan as this would create too much detail – these will be generated as the rider progresses through the year to allow for training to be adjusted to the specific conditions that he or she faces at the time.

Notice that the rider's year does not begin on 1st January! Preparation has to begin much earlier than that for the successful cyclist – especially one wishing to do well at a high level.

YEAR PLANNER

MESOCYCLE	RECOVERY MESOCYCLE	PREPARATION MESO-CYCLE #1	PREPARATION MESO-CYCLE #2	PREPARATION MESO-CYCLE #3	TRANSITION MESO-CYCLE PRIOR TO RACING	RACING MESO-CYCLE #1	RACING MESO-CYCLE #2	RACING MESO-CYCLE #3
ACTIVITY	Easy rides	Progressive build-up of long, steady distance rides. Progressive work on strength & areas of weakness			Speed training (anaerobic)	Racing. Progressively longer distances and greater intensity, interspersed with short-distance speed work and rest		
						MINOR PEAK	**MAJOR EVENT**	
						▼	▼	
TRAINING ZONE	Zones 1–2	Mainly Zones 1–2, occasionally Zone 3			Mostly training in Zones 3–6	Racing in Zones 4–6 Training in Zones 3–6 Tapering to peak for specific goals towards the end of each meso-cycle with recovery week after each peak		
TRAINING PHASE	Recovery	Preparation			Pre-comp	Competition		
MONTH	OCT	NOV	DEC	JAN	FEB	MAR	APR	MAY	JUN	JUL	AUG	SEP

Calculating training load

You will see the sample training plan refers to training zones – put simply, this gives the rider an idea of how much effort, or intensity, they should put in to each session.

One simple method of calculating your intensity of effort is to use a rating of perceived exertion (RPE). This is a well-established method that is used in many sports and is based on the Borg Scale – a simplified version of this is given below. It is subjective but the numbers you use are just to compare one ride or training session with another, so the subjectivity is fine.

You can use smaller increments, taking the RPE to one decimal place, to fine tune the description of effort if necessary.

Not only will the RPE be useful to show you exactly how much effort you need to put into a session, but you can also use it to compare sessions and calculate overall effort. You can do this by taking your RPE and multiplying it by the duration of the session. For example: a session at RPE 5 which lasts for two hours would give you a figure of 600 (5 x 120 minutes), whereas a session at RPE 7 which only lasted 45 minutes would give you a figure of 315 (7 x 45).

You can then record these daily figures on a graph, and this will quickly highlight when you have periods of 'excessive exercise' which will require more rest afterwards.

Cyclo-cross requires good flexibility for the frequent hops off the bike, among other fitness components.

VERY VERY LIGHT	LIGHT	MODERATE	SOMEWHAT HEAVY	HEAVY OR HARD	HEAVY +	VERY HEAVY	VERY HEAVY +	VERY HEAVY ++	VERY VERY HEAVY
1	2	3	4	5	6	7	8	9	10

Adaptation

As you progress through the months of cycling, you will adapt your fitness (muscular and cardiovascular) to suit your needs. This is essential development of fitness for purpose'. If your goal is to be a faster long-distance racing cyclist, then your training will have to include some faster, shorter rides and not just riding long distances at a steady pace. Pursuit riders on the track will practise their starts and short distances at much greater speeds than they can expect to maintain over 4,000m (2.5mi.) in a race. Cyclo-cross riders and mountain-bikers need to perfect their bike handling skills at speed and even short distance time-triallists can benefit from training at higher cadences and speeds over shorter distances than their competition distances.

Progression

Your muscles, heart and lungs (and backside) need to be introduced to the demands of cycling over a period of time. If you do too much too soon, you will feel over-tired and find yourself overtrained (see below). If you do the same training every week, every year, you will plateau at a level and not get any fitter (see *Variation*, below). This is a typical problem faced by many amateur racers who repeat their training patterns year after year but fail to improve their performances. You need to vary and progress your riding, so that your body is pushed a little harder if you wish to become fitter. You can do this by riding more often, for longer, or by riding faster.

Variation

Do the same training all the time and you'll probably be quite good at that style of riding – provided you're not overtrained or bored to numbness by it. But you will reach a level and have a limited repertoire of skills and speed.

There are few aspects of cycling which require just one style of riding: road racers, mountain bikers and cyclo-cross riders need stamina to last the duration of the event, climbing and descending, sprinting, cornering and bunch riding skills. The off-road riders need additional skills to cope with the terrain and to mount and dismount their bikes quickly. Track riders need to be able to accelerate and ride tactically and even time-triallists need to cope with different terrains, weather conditions and pace judgement for different courses.

To be a competent bike rider you need to practise all the aspects you might find in your chosen area of the sport (see *Chapter 2*). You can bring variation into your training by riding different routes, incorporating on and off-road riding, using a variety of exercises to cover speed, endurance and skills. Change the duration and intensity of sessions too and be sure to include periods of rest or, at least, some easier sessions from time to time.

Overload

Overload is necessary to build your body up to cope with the stresses and demands you are going to put on it. When Chris Boardman set his world hour record distance for the one hour track event in 1996, his overload training was riding the three-week Tour de France shortly beforehand. He then came 'up to speed' with a brief recovery period and six weeks of fast, short-distance training to bring him to the level needed.

Your overload training could be one or two weeks high-mileage cycling holiday or a training camp, 3–6 weeks before a big stage race or before a 12-hour time trial. You must allow time to recover from the overload to avoid being tired when you begin your target event.

Be prepared to work hard in training to overload...

And beware that there is a fine line between overload and over-training.

Over-training, rest and recovery

More is not always better. If you exercise without enough time to rest and recover you will become fatigued, leading to poor performances. Over-training is characterised by:

- chronic injury or infection
- fatigue and unexpected sense of effort during training
- unexplained loss of performance
- heavy, stiff or sore muscles
- slow recovery
- greater incidence of infection
- disturbed sleep
- mood swings or irritability
- loss of energy, motivation, libido or appetite.

...but be sure to get plenty of rest.

Over-training is surprisingly common – it is easy to get into the mindset that you must do more and more in order to improve, and that rest days are opportunities wasted. As we have seen when looking at muscles (above) we must rest in order to build improved muscle fibre, so remind yourself that rest is an essential part of your training programme and is equally as important as any other session in your plan.

There are a number of steps you can take to ensure that you avoid over-training:

- ensure adequate carbohydrate intake before and during exercise
- vary training intensities, activities and locations
- reduce psychological stress
- reduce exposure to over-heating
- have a balanced diet
- avoid excessive training volumes
- control the rate of progression of training
- allow adequate recovery time between sessions.

The sooner you begin eating after exercise, the quicker you can replenish muscle glycogen and be ready for the next activity. Aim to eat within the first two hours after exercise, as carbohydrate is absorbed at a quicker rate than at other times.

Reversibility

This lies at the other extreme to over-training. In other words, 'use It, or lose it'. If you stop training, you will revert to your untrained state. You will lose strength, speed, stamina and flexibility. In simple terms, you lose aerobic endurance gains in about a third of the time that it takes to build them up whereas strength diminishes at a slower rate, and even skill levels will drop off if riders do not practise them. This is one reason why pursuit riders, despite a solid foundation of endurance and speed usually gained from a season of road racing, spend a great deal of time honing their track craft again before major championships.

Reversibility is another reason why returning after holidays, comebacks after a lay-off or an injury should be started at an easy level and progressed gradually (see *Progression* above) to ease the muscles and motor skills back up to speed, rather than trying to recommence training from the level when the inactivity began.

Choosing your races

Introduction

The previous two chapters have enabled you to analyse your skills and your fitness to determine which cycling discipline(s) best suits you. The logical next step is to look in more detail each to see if you actually want to ride in the events that suit you! In this chapter we look at each of the main cycling disciplines, give an overview of the events that each contains, provide points to help you if you are starting out and give you some more detailed tactical and strategic advice if you are beyond that stage but still struggling to make an impact on the racing scene.

If you are approaching your cycling from the other direction – i.e. you've picked your discipline before you work on the required fitness and skills mix – then it's worth taking a few minutes to read these sections to make sure that you know what you are getting yourself into.

It's also worth noting that although this chapter looks primarily at racing in each discipline, all the advice – with the possible exception of strategies – applies equally whether you take to the roads, the track or the trails for a bit of weekend relaxation. Cycling really is one of those sports where it never hurts to be prepared.

Road racing

Road riding and, by extension, road racing is the traditional cycling discipline, if for no other reason that everybody has access to tarmac roads to ride on. From this popularity it also follows that the discipline gets the most media coverage and television time which in turn leads to huge events – most notably the Tour De France – and this attracts more people to the discipline.

It's often possible to fit road riding into a daily routine to commute to college or work and this is an excellent use of time for training or just general fitness.

The main events

Most road races are 'one day' races, anything from 10km (6.25mi.) for youth or junior riders to over 250km (150+mi.) for some of the Classic races contested by the top professional teams on the Continent. But don't worry if you don't feel up to that yet, for adult novices a typical road race will be around 50–60km (30–37.5mi.).

Criteriums are held around tight circuits in town or city centres. They usually last no more than one hour plus a lap. The short laps mean that riders have to be proficient at entering and exiting corners. A few intermediate sprints ('primes'), with the prospect of some prize money, guarantee a fast pace. The good thing here is that you'll never be far from the action, even if you've been lapped by faster, more experienced riders. (Lapped riders may be withdrawn from the race in its closing stages.)

There are closed-road circuits, which are (usually) well-surfaced with the bonus of being completely traffic-free. Many are specifically designed for cycle racing and so have sweeping bends which can be ridden at speed (whereas criterium courses in town centres often have 90 degree – or sharper – corners with drains and kerbs to negotiate and usually require use of the brakes and a sprint to get back up to speed). The bonus for local riders is that they can often use the circuit for training, and regular racing (most circuits run summer evening or weekend racing leagues) will soon develop familiarity and confidence on the circuit.

Stage races are probably the most well-known of all cycle races. These are a number of individual road races linked together, either to form a loop such as the Tour de France, Giro d'Italia or Tour of Britain, or they may be stages based around one location such as the Surrey 5-day. Most stage races commence with a prologue time trial to rank the riders in the General Classification, and there may be another individual time trial or team time trial on other days. The overall winner is the rider with the lowest aggregate time of all the stages, and there are usually other prizes for 'King of the Mountains', sprints and points (a prize awarded for consistent placings across the various prize categories) and each individual stage. Teamwork plays a significant role in stage races, with the best riders helped and protected by their team-mates so that they can contest the prizes – which are then often shared amongst the team.

MAJOR ROAD RACES IN THE WORLD

The three Grand Tours (Tour de France, Giro d'Italia, Vuelta a España) sit at the pinacle of road racing. Beneath them are a number of shorter stage races — the Dauphiné Libéré and Tour of Switzerland are traditional 'warm-ups' for riders competing in the Tour de France and the early season Paris-Nice (the 'Race to the Sun') is always keenly contested as an indicator as to who has been training hard over the winter.

CLASSICS
A handful of top one-day road races held in the spring and autumn have earned the cachet of 'Classic'.

The Northern Classics:
- Het Volk is the traditional season opener.
- Ghent-Welvelgem is not part of the UCI's World Cup but still attracts a class field as it is held in the week between the following.
- Tour of Flanders is renowned for its relentless 'bergs' (short, steep climbs) in the second half.
- Paris-Roubaix, the brutal 'Queen of the Classics', also known as the 'Hell of the North', takes riders across some of the worst roads in northern France. Many are cobbled and some are no more than farm tracks, thick with slippery mud in wet conditions and choking with dust in the dry.

The other Classics are Liège-Bastogne-Liège ('La Doyenne', first run in 1892), Fleche Wallone in the Ardennes and Holland's only Classic, the Amstel Gold. Every Italian's dream event is Milan-San Remo held in the spring. The professional season closes with autumn's Paris-Tours and the Tour of Lombardy in Italy.

The UK's Premier Calendar is a season-long competition of the major one-day races, including: the Archer Grand Prix, Lincoln Grand Prix and the Tour of the Peak.

WOMEN'S RACING
The women's calendar is less established than the men's so events are rather more ephemeral. The Tour Féminin is a shortened version of the Tour de France and the Giro d'Italia Femminile is Italy's equivalent major stage race. Third on the women's international calendar is the 10-day Tour de l'Aude in south west France. A number of the Classics also feature women's versions now as part of a season-long World Cup competition just like the men's, and there is a healthy women's scene in the US.

Find a 'good wheel' to follow – Greg Lemond is one of the best and even the pros will take his lead.

Starting out

The initial twenty minutes of your first road race event are a critical time. Do the right thing and you can save yourself a lot of wasted effort and you'll enjoy it a lot more. And you might even come back for more.

Be aware that it's pretty rare that you will win your first road race. Experience will not be on your side. Unfortunately, this is why a fair share of riders do just one race and never return. The first rule to learn in road racing is that you need to be patient.

There are a couple of obvious basic rules that you should know before taking on your first road race or, indeed, any race: safety and awareness. Beyond this, the two fundamentals of road racing are bunch riding and chasing. Know a bit about these before you line up behind your first start line and you will save yourself a whole lot of effort, and pain.

Safety

Safety is paramount. Racing on the open roads is a potentially dangerous activity – even closed roads and circuits can offer problems. The commissaire, or chief judge, will usually brief the riders beforehand on what is expected of them during the race. He or she will run through the course and let riders know of any changes to the route, dangerous corners, etc. Their word is final, so pay attention.

Remember that you also need to be responsible for other riders. You may be competing against them, but safety is a shared interest and winning is never worth it if you achieve it by putting others at risk. As you improve, you will find yourself being involved with the peloton – lots of people travelling at high speed with little room for error. In these situations, safety is a group concern.

Stay alert

The start of the race is when most people feel frisky and full of riding, so there will be various attacks and chases followed by huge variations in speed and general messing about. There is never any pattern to this part of the race, so it's not really a surprise that very few of the riders will have a clue what to do – and the general chaos often sends inexperienced riders into further confusion and panic.

During the early minutes of your first race you'll be worrying about the close riding of the bunch and concentrating pretty hard on where your front wheel is going. At this point, for at least a third of the bunch, survival seems like the main objective, rather than winning. It is easy to say, but stay calm – this way you will take in information about the race and be in a position to react to, or even anticipate, any moves in or around the bunch.

Bunch riding

This is both the most enticing and daunting part of road racing – riding 'wheel to wheel' with a number of other riders at pace. Whether you are in the lead group or further down the race, bunch riding will make your race easier and more enjoyable.

Many riders new to bunch riding tend to overdo everything, accelerating too much as they reach the front or trying to get off the front too quickly – most of this activity is unnecessary and wastes valuable energy. For example, if you are riding in two lines (moving through on the right) the left-hand string will be 'soft pedalling' in order to drift to the back. So to get through to the front you just need to 'roll through', allowing enough space for the front rider before you swing over.

The problems start when people upset this tempo and ride for themselves or without thinking, surging through too fast and breaking up the line of riders behind them. This forces the riders behind to chase the gaps left by the acceleration – if you do this, you'll soon struggle to find friends in the peloton.

The best advice for your first couple of experiences of bunch riding is to accept your inexperience and take the lead of the wiser heads around you – in most situations they will be more than happy to guide you in the right direction.

See group riding in *Chapter 2* for more guidance on the skills that you will need.

Making sense of the chaos

Unless there is a team structure, the usual amateur road race bunch remains fairly chaotic from start to finish. The structure and organisation of the bunch depends on:

1. The direction and strength of the wind.
2. The number of riders wanting to help.
3. The overall size of the bunch.
4. The ability and experience of the riders.

You will quickly pick up the knowledge and experience to make judgement calls on all these issues, and could well find yourself becoming the 'leader' who brings order to things. But this takes time. Until then, it is better to 'volunteer your services' and be led by more experienced riders.

When do I pull?

The accepted cycling etiquette is to contribute an appropriate effort ('pull your weight') at the front of any group, but this can mean you risk damaging your own chances of winning, or even completing, the race. By all means, take a turn at the front and move back into the comfort of the bunch, but to start with stay tucked away among the other riders' wheels and out of the wind. Avoid the temptation to get drawn into the 'action' at the front – leading an attack or bridging across to a breakaway group may seem like you are 'racing' but really all you are doing is reducing your chances of success. So don't do it.

This is the classic mistake for triathletes, mountain bikers and time triallists new to the road racing game. They go straight to the front, showing off how strong they are, and everyone else sits behind them enjoying the ride and waiting for them to get tired. If you have good strong legs, why are you wasting all that energy? Wait for your moment nearer the finish line.

Chasing

The biggest issue you face physically is the fact you will have to close gaps on your own back and forth like a rubber band – sometimes known as 'bouncing the elastic'. Over time this becomes more fatiguing and harder to do. That's when the elastic snaps. At the back of the bunch you will be working harder, far harder, than a rider in the first ten places. If you can hang on to the back of the bunch, you should be thinking about moving up as soon as you can.

Staying at the back has three basic 'my race is nearly over' issues:

1. You will have to make more frequent and harder efforts to chase the bunch after corners or any increases in pace.
2. You are far more likely to get tangled up in splits and crashes.
3. The race is all happening far away at the head of the field and you'll miss all the action and fun.

The 'schoolboy error' chase

If a break goes down the road the usual technique is for two or three riders to chase it down. Often even they don't know why, like dogs chasing sticks, they just want to... then the break is caught and everyone sits up. This is pointless and terribly frustrating for the breakaway group as they are probably trying to make a gap and working hard together to stay away. Then, once the contact is made, there may be another breakaway and the process continues until the willing riders are exhausted and the final attack stays put, or the bunch is still all together for an almighty sprint for the finish line.

This is typical of beginner racing and can make the racing very negative. You'll notice in pro racing that it's rare for riders to chase a break straight away. They usually let things develop and if a team wants it to work they will shut down the chase or, if they don't have a rider in the move, they send someone over to the break (bridging). All these things are pre-arranged or decided on the road by the team leader. The teams without a rider there, or those with the strongest sprinters looking for a bunch sprint, will always be expected to organise the chase. Rarely do the big name riders get into breaks early on because they will be saving their legs for the final section.

As a new rider you can learn from this. There will be plenty of riders who haven't read this book and will be happy to chase and do all the hard work early on in the race, thinking that they are heir apparent to Lance Armstrong or Tom Boonen. Take advantage of this by letting those riders wear themselves out. This way there will be fewer riders to trouble you later on in the event.

Pushing on

Once you have the first few races under your belt you can move your mindset from 'complete the distance' to 'compete in the race'. You can get more involved in the cut and thrust of the race and will find yourself moving up the field. And you may be surprised to find that this actually makes the riding easier and not harder.

There are countless strategies within road racing – it's like chess but with more players – but there are a couple of key points that are worth highlighting: how to plan a tactical race and how to attack.

Tactics

Your tactics for a race will be a combination of proactive and reactive strategies – some of these you will have to work on before the race, and others will have to be made up as you ride.

First of all, ask yourself some questions during the race:
- who is strong?
- who is happy to work, relentlessly?
- who is aggressive, but weak in the breaks?
- who is happy to follow wheels?
- who looks like they've done this before?

It is all about information gathering – you will be able to use this both during the race and in future races against the same riders and teams. This really does keep you focused and can help to take your mind off your aching legs.

Then after the race, ask these questions:
- what happened to the key riders as the race progressed?
- where did these key riders finish?
- what did you think the winner had that you didn't?

Once you've considered all information from the race, at your next race make an effort to follow the experienced wheels and avoid the less confident ones (as they are more likely to get caught in the wrong place or, worse still, cause or become involved in a crash). The riders attacking and trying to get away may well get a few metres off the front but usually the (over)enthusiastic behind will chase all of the early breaks down. This is because the riders in these breakaway groups are either not committed enough to the move or just don't have the legs for it.

Remember to watch again for the strongest riders and those who are just along for the ride, as this will help you develop a strategy for later in the race. For the complete novice there is a tendency to be pushed to the back of the bunch where it appears to be calmer and less confusing. This can be your first mistake...

Attack

Attacking, climbing and sprinting have a great deal in common – the good climbers often make good sprinters, as both require explosive effort. For more details of the mechanics of these skills plus the physical attributes that you will need, see *Chapters 2* and *3*.

Sprinting can be daunting, exhausting and tactical. Track riders learn these techniques as a matter of course – if you struggle when the bunch hits the final kilometre then get down to the track, it will help you to develop your sprinting in no time like Mario Cippolini, Eric Zabel or Tom Boonen.

Breaking away alone requires a massive effort and staying off the front of a fast moving peleton is unspeakably difficult.

Attack as if you mean it – a gap will soon develop if your timing is right.

At its most basic, you need to know:

- how to get into position
- when to attack
- where to attack
- how to attack.

Moving up

Once you've done a few races you'll need to learn how to get around the peloton quickly and smoothly. This is the hard part. On the open road you also need to consider traffic and other road users.

If you imagine the peloton as being a flock of birds, there will be fluid parts of the flock and more rigid parts. The outside flanks are usually the fluid parts. In the same way a road racing bunch has riders hovering around its edges, constantly aiming to join the chain of riders to get up to the front. Once at the front you can either drift back, or maintain your position – it's a constant flow as you move forward. When planning an attack you need to stay at the front, so this means you have to find the solid part of the peloton, where you know you can sit happily – 'Armstrong style' – surveying the race ahead of you.

However, in the Tour de France any team leader would use his team-mates to help hold his position – they fetch and carry stuff, keep a check on breaks, chase unwelcome gaps and 'ride shotgun' to protect him from poor moves from other riders or to prevent other riders sitting behind his back wheel. He still has to retain his position, but it's much easier when that's all you have to think about.

When to attack

Most attacks are launched when there is a lull in the action – perhaps after a break has been caught, just after a sprint lap or as a strong rider has just had a go at creating a gap. These are all times when everyone is using the slowing down as a bit of a breather. Some riders will keep attacking relentlessly after each move has returned and this is a good tactic if you have the legs for it. Eventually the bunch will give up chasing you and you'll be away.

Where to attack

There are no set rules to this, but hills are always a good bet. Attacking on a windy day, into the wind, may seem a little stupid (and it usually is) but it can work. However, solo breaks on windy days rarely succeed, so unless you can persuade a few others out of the comfort of the peloton, then it's better to stay put and wait.

Some races can be won by attacking on a slippery corner that other riders are hesitant on, or on a downhill section. The key is to work out where you plan to get an advantage and then prepare for that moment.

Once a gap is established, check back to assess the damage – have they decided to let you go or has a group joined you in the break?

The 'where' is all about your tactics – know your strengths, know the course and, where possible, know your opponents.

How to attack

This one's simple: Go for it! Don't look back and don't hold back until you have established a significant gap. Work like a Trojan if you have to – and you will need to – if you want the move to stick. You can ease up a little when the break is away, but the biggest mistake you can make is not committing everything to it in the first instance. Half-hearted attacks are pointless – and they never succeed. Once you've jumped you need to accelerate as quickly as you can and bury yourself in 100% effort for at least 500m, perhaps even a kilometre. Then, sneak a look behind you – if no-one has reacted, keep going. If two or three riders have reacted, ease up very slightly and let them catch you. Working together you'll be a much more efficient machine and better able to stay away from the bunch.

Track racing

Track racing is a paradoxical discipline – it is both the simplest and the most complicated form of cycle racing. The bikes are really simple and some of the racing is also pretty simple – pursuits and sprints are pure one-against-one, first across the line events. However, in races like the Madison, Points Race and the Devil there are complicated rules and tactics.

Once you've ridden the track for the first time, you will wish you had started doing it earlier. It's a great workout, it's exhilarating and it's great fun.

The main events

Track racing is essentially divided into two categories: endurance and sprint events. The myth about track riders is that they are all big, hefty riders with huge legs and that power is their only concern. Some sprinters do like the gym (possibly a bit too much) but most of the endurance riders are essentially road riders. One thing is certain; good track riders make excellent road riders as they have natural speed and tactical sense.

1km Time Trial

This is about as simple as it gets. Riders race one-by-one against the clock from a standing start position, held upright by starting gate. Then it's four laps of the 250m (0.2mi.) track as fast as you can possibly go. The Women's race is held over 500 metres (0.3mi.).

A good benchmark time would be 1 minute 10 seconds for men and inside 40 seconds for women.

The sprint is a tactical race – and not for the feint hearted.

Essential skills required: A fast start, a good aero-tuck position and a strong finish without fading.

Sprint

This race is a little harder to follow. In big competitions riders will first complete a 200m (0.1mi.) time trial to determine the fastest 16. The competition will be organised into specific matches. What follows is a series of heats and repechages where the final eight riders emerge. From the quarter-finals onwards, two-up matches over two heats (and a third deciding heat, if necessary) take place with the winners progressing to the semi-finals. Quarter-final losers will ride a four-up sprint for places five to eight. In World and Olympic championships, the two winners of the semi-finals will compete for the first and second place and the two losers of the semi-finals for the third and fourth.

Essential skills required: Positional sense, balance and technique for stand stills (waiting for the first 'move'), plenty of nerve for control at high speeds, powerful arms and upper body for added power, and explosive, assertive tactics.

Scratch racing adopts many of the tactics of road racers, including the lead out for the sprint by team-mates.

Scratch Race

Basically, this is a road race on the track. Usually held over 10, 15, 20 or 25km. Many track sprinters can do well here, as long as they can hang on to the fast-moving bunch. Riders with less of a finish may try to escape and build a breakaway, which can change the shape of the race, with riders chasing and pulling back the attack.

Essential skills required: Endurance, a good final sprint, and attacking sense should a break or opportunity to get clear arise.

Individual Pursuit

This is basically a match sprint for endurance riders. First a qualifying round will select the eight fastest riders over a distance of 4km (2.5mi.) (3km (1.9mi.) for women and juniors). The four winners of the first round go through to the finals. The faster rider is the winner of each individual round. The secret is riding fast enough to qualify but not so fast as to over-cook it for the later round. However, the riders with the two best times ride for the first and second place, while the two other riders ride for third and fourth places, which prevents any 'coasting' in the qualifying round. The riders start on opposite sides (home and back straight) of the track.

> ## WORLD RECORDS – INDIVIDUAL PURSUIT
>
> The world records for the Individual Pursuit are currently held by Britain's Chris Boardman with a time of 4 minutes 11.114 seconds (1996) and by Sarah Ulmer of New Zealand in 3 minutes 24.537 seconds (2004 Olympics). Michael Ford of Australia has the Junior record with a time of 3 minutes 17.775 (2004).

Essential skills required: A good start, a high sustainable 'cruising' speed, and the ability to ride to a schedule and judge effort levels.

Points Race

Points are won during the intermediate lap and the final lap sprints and by winning or 'taking' laps (by lapping the main bunch). The intermediate sprints occur every ten laps and points are usually awarded:

- · 5 points to the first rider
- · 3 points to the second
- · 2 points to the third
- · 1 point to the fourth.

In addition, a rider who manages to gain a lap on the main bunch gets 20 points.

In big competitions, riders will cover a total distance of 40km (160 laps). You have to pay attention, as with plenty of lapping and attempted lapping going on there's always some confusion as to who is on which lap.

Essential skills required: Power in the sprint, good leg speed, endurance for attacks and taking laps, concentration, and tactical sense.

A points race needs all-round ability – power in the sprints and endurance.

Changeovers in the Madison can be pretty dangerous, but impressive to watch!

Madison

The Madison (which originated at Madison Square Garden, New York) is *the* race of the European six-day circuit.

You have to concentrate very hard on what is going on as it can get confusing, but this can be the most exciting of all the track events. Teams of two riders will compete in a race run over a distance of 50km (31mi.) (200 laps) with several intermediate sprints thrown in. The 'resting riders' circle the track above the blue stayer's line as the race goes on below it. To get the resting rider up to speed and into the action the changeover is done with a 'hand sling' where the racing rider literally takes the hand of the resting rider and pulls him into the race and throws him forward up to speed (at the same time, arresting his own speed) into the race.

Teams can take laps (lap the field), so those teams having covered the same number of laps at the finish will be placed according to their accumulated points. Where there is a draw on both laps and points, the number of wins in the sprints decides the final result. Sprint points will be awarded as in the Points Race (see page 99).

When a Madison race is reaching its climax it can be a thrilling event and when done well, the skill levels shown are mind-boggling. Choreography is required between the riders to avoid one another as half the field are speeding up and the other half are slowing down.

Essential skills required: Hand slings need plenty of practice, endurance skills, tactical sense and positional awareness, and experience.

Devil Takes the Hindmost

This is another somewhat bizarre event, especially to the uninitiated track spectator. The 'Devil', as it is often known, is usually run over 30–50 laps depending on the size of the field. The bunch rides around and at the end of each lap the last rider over the line is pulled out by the judges. This means that there is usually a sprint towards the back of the bunch to prevent being eliminated. The race continues with one rider being pulled out each lap until there are six (or maybe fewer) remaining. Then they will be given a few laps to race for the finish line. It's fun to do, mad to watch and always a tricky one for the judges.

Essential skills required: Positional sense, track skills, a good turn of speed, and a sprint when it's needed.

Team Pursuit

Two teams of four riders compete against each other in a 4km (2.5mi.) race, starting from the middle of the straight of each side of the track. The winner is determined by either catching the other team or recording the fastest time, which is recorded when the front tyre of the teams' third rider crosses the line. A qualifying round, where each team competes alone on the track, will select the eight best teams on the basis of their time, in order to compete in the first round. The four winners of the first round contest the finals. The teams with the two best times ride for the first and second place, while the other two teams ride for third and fourth place.

WORLD RECORDS – TEAM PURSUIT

The world record for the Team Pursuit is held by Australia and is an incredible 3 minutes 56.610 seconds, set at the 2004 Olympics.

Essential skills required: Ability to ride close and with tight control in the changeovers – a team needs to be well matched and individuals need plenty of endurance power.

Team Sprint

Experienced riders can easily get up to 60kph (37.5mph) in this event and it's all over in under 45 seconds. Two teams of three riders will run over three laps of the track, with each rider leading for one lap before peeling off one at a time to leave the last rider to complete the third and final lap. A qualifying round, run by heats, will select the eight best teams on the basis of their times, in order for them to compete in the first round. The four winners of the first round contest the finals. The teams with the two best times ride for the first and second place, while the other two teams ride for third and fourth place.

Essential skills required: Sheer speed, the ability to ride close and with tight control in the changeovers – a team needs to be well matched and very powerful. The standing start also takes some skill.

Keirin

Follow the derny until it leaves the track, and then anything goes!

This is a bit like a demolition derby (without the cars and the carnage, of course). Invented in Japan, where they use this event for gambling, 'Keirin' translates as 'fight' and it's certainly not for the faint hearted. Riders compete in a sprint after completing a certain number of laps behind a motorised pacer (derny), who leaves the track 600–700m (0.3–0.4mi.) before the finish. The pacer will start at 30kph (18.75mph) and gradually increases the speed to over 50kph (31.25mph), before leaving the track. Following a specific composition table, 21 riders will compete in three heats of seven riders, during the first round, and two heats of six riders, during the second round. The three winners of each heat of the second round will proceed to the final, for places one–six, while the rest will race for places seven–twelve.

The main aim is to be close to the wheel of the derny where there is more shelter from the wind and you can command the race once it has swung away. It's fair to say that apart from not taking your hands off the handlebars, pretty much anything goes in this race and riders will use shoulders, elbows and helmets to muscle into place ready for the final sprint. The judges aren't always sympathetic with dangerous changes of direction and underhand tactics, but it is an incredible event to watch!

Essential skills required: High cadence, nerves of steel, the ability to push onto the wheel of the bike, to unleash an explosive sprint and also a little endurance can help too.

The one hour record

This is the Blue Riband event of track cycling and many great names in cycling have taken it on – Jacques Anquetil, Fausto Coppi and Francesco Moser to name a few. The event is straightforward – it simply comes down to how far you can ride in one hour on the track.

Henri Desgrange, the founder of the Tour de France, set the first figures in 1893 and he managed 35,325m (22mi.). The 'Absolute Hour Record' was set by Chris Boardman at 56, 375m (35mi.) in 1996. The International Cycling Union (UCI) then took control of the technical development of the event and decided that technical assistance from aerodynamic positions and equipment should be limited. Essentially they reset the technical specification of the bike you could use (apart from the pedals) back to 1972 when the great Eddy Merckx set the record at altitude in Mexico (49,432m 30.7mi.). This became known as the 'Athlete's Record'. The figures were reset by Chris Boardman at Manchester in 2000, just prior to his retirement who added just 10m (32ft.) to Merckx's distance.

The record is currently held by Czech rider Ondrej Sosenka with 49,700 m (30.9mi.) in 2005. The women's record is held by French cycling legend, Jeannie Longo-Ciprelli with 45,094m (28mi.) in 2000.

Essential skills required: Enormous cardio-vascular resources with the added ability to suffer, a lot. A smooth pedalling style – suits time trial and pursuit riders.

Note the angle of the track and the various coloured lines.

Starting out
When you take to the track for the first time, there are a few things that you need to be aware of – not least of which is the track itself.

The track
Tracks (velodromes) are either indoor or outdoor. Indoor tracks are usually wooden and 250m (0.2mi.) for one lap. Outdoor tracks are usually concrete or tarmac and have less steeply banked curves and are usually wider than indoor ones. This means that they can be better for larger fields of riders. All tracks have drop-in sessions that allow you to ride at your own pace and level under the watchful eye of a coach. There are also league meetings for when you feel confident enough to start racing.

On an indoor track, the blue strip around the bottom of the track is where you will be lapping at first – it's romantically known as the Côte d'Azure. This will get you the feel for the boards and the coach will explain at this point that they want you to get used to the fixed gear and to feel comfortable on the bike. In time, you will perhaps ride onto the straights and back onto the blue for the corners, and you'll also be picking up speed. Eventually you will move up towards the black datum line and onto the track itself. Most riders will be riding laps on the track within an hour or so and riding in groups soon after.

The force is with you
The banking on a track is there so you can go very fast without sliding out on the corners. There are various forces at work to help a rider stay upright around a track. Gravity pushes the rider down into the track, and the reaction force of the track itself pushes back against the bike. As the rider turns, if the track was not banked, the bike would slip away from underneath with unequal forces acting on the bike's tyres. The banking on a track actually assists you in going faster, more safely. You can also use it to help accelerate for tactical advantage and to slow down. All in all, track riding is a lot safer than road or mountain biking.

At any point, the banking is the same angle all the way to the top of the track, although this may vary between the straights, transitions and the bankings themselves. Yes, you are higher up but the grip of your tyres is the same and the angle of the bike identical to when you are on the bottom.

TRAINING ON THE TRACK

The track is the best place to train intensively, no matter what your discipline. A good two hour session will put you through some highly beneficial workouts, you will have a coach watching you and giving advice, and the fixed gear bikes really develop your pedalling technique.

Fixed gear riding is an excellent way to develop pedalling 'souplesse' and is mandatory on the track.

Fixed gear riding

Track bikes have a single fixed gear (no freewheel like road or mountain bikes), so you have to keep pedalling at all times. This is not as hard as it sounds and the natural instinct is to keep the pedals turning, as not only do you maintain momentum but pedalling also helps your balance. You do get used to it very quickly though and even if you do forget you usually only get a slight 'kick' from the pedals, which will be enough to remind you to start pedalling again.

I've got no brakes!

Moving up the banking increases the lap length and therefore slows you down in relation to others if you are riding in a group. When riders are tightly packed together it would be carnage to start braking. Easing off and back slightly on the pedals, or moving up the track, will subtly decrease your speed and still allow you to ride closely to the wheels of other riders.

You will find that you develop a 'sixth sense' of speed control and it really teaches you a thing or two about maintaining a smooth and rounded pedal stroke. As with all bike riding skills, the first thing to do is to relax your shoulders without gripping the handlebars too tightly.

Pushing on

The best advice we can give to more experienced riders seeking better results is to get as much track time for training and competition as possible and to find a coach who can give you personal training, reflecting your abilities and ambitions.

Here are a few pointers that you should bear in mind whenever you ride on the track.
- Do not watch the tyre of the rider in front of you, instead focus further ahead – this keeps your head up and allows you to see what's happening down the track.
- Keep your speed at a reasonable pace, this is the key to staying on the banking – slow down and gravity will start to push down the track and you can lose grip.
- Look where you want to go – towards the top of the banking and around the corner, rather than at the base of the track, to avoid drifting off the track.
- Look over your shoulder to ensure that it is safe to move before you do so.
- Make sure you keep pressure on the pedals when riding through the bankings.
- Always obey the coach – do what they say and you will be fine.

Time trialling

Time trials are probably the most accessible races for most cyclists in the UK. Many clubs hold regular, informal 'club' events and are pleased to welcome other local riders. These events are usually held over 16 or 40km (10 or 25 mil.), either on a Sunday morning or weekday evening.

Clubs also promote 'open' events, over any distance from 16km to 160km (10 mi. to 100 mil.), and a few promote events at 12 and 24 hours in the latter half of the season. In between, there are 'association' events for members of clubs affiliated to the association. There is a growing trend towards non-standard distance events, over hilly 'sporting' courses. The British Time Trial Championship (BTTC) is a combined promotion between British Cycling and Cycling Time Trials which tests riders over hilly, non-standard distances – much like Continental time trials.

In a time trial, riders race alone. For many, the challenge is to beat their 'personal best' (PB) over the distance – although that may be largely dependent on the road, traffic and weather conditions – or perhaps to beat a club-mate or rival. Even if you prefer other cycling disciplines, time trials are an excellent way to test and measure your fitness, so it's worth doing a few during the season to check how you're going.

The main events

Races over 16km and 40km (10 and 25 mi.) are the mainstay of time trialling, and for that they are most cyclists' introduction to competitive cycling. Any rider over the age of 12 can compete in time trials on the open highway.

The top riders can usually get close to, or even under, 20 minutes for 16km (10 mi.) and 50 minutes for 40km (25 mi.) (30mph or 48kmph), although 24 minutes and 1 hour (25mph or 40kmph) respectively are more reasonable goals for the average club cyclist.

Team time trials are popular, often as early season events with two or three riders ('2-up' or '3-up') but sometimes as a four person team. Sometimes held in the Tour de France there are full teams of nine riders, which is spectacular to watch as they all fly by in unison like a powerful locomotive.

The records
To give you an idea of how the pros get on, here are the current world records.

MEN'S

DISTANCE (OR TIME) OF EVENT	RIDER	TIME (OR DISTANCE) ACHIEVED	YEAR SET
16KM (10 MILE)	STUART DANGERFIELD	00:18:19	2001
40KM (25 MILE)	CHRIS BOARDMAN, MBE	00:45:57	1993
80KM (50 MILE)	KEVIN DAWSON	01:37:21	1997
160KM (100 MILE)	KEVIN DAWSON	03:22:45	2003
12 HOUR	ANDY WILKINSON	300.27mi.	1996
24 HOUR	ANDY WILKINSON	525.07mi.	1997

WOMEN'S

DISTANCE (OR TIME) OF EVENT	RIDER	TIME (OR DISTANCE) ACHIEVED	YEAR SET
16KM (10 MILE)	MAXINE JOHNSON	00:20:38	1993
40KM (25 MILE)	YVONNE MCGREGOR	00:51:50	1996
80KM (50 MILE)	JILL REAMES	01:47:48	1997
160KM (100 MILE)	JENNY DERHAM	03:53:04	1996
12 HOUR	BERYL BURTON, MBE	277.25mi.	1967
24 HOUR	CHRISTINE ROBERTS	461.45mi.	1993

Essential skills

The skills that you will require will depend on the distance and duration that you are trialling:

- 16–40km (10–25 mi.) – thorough warm-up, rapid start, all out effort close to the anaerobic threshold, maintaining an aerodynamic position
- 80–160km (50–100 mi.) – good warm-up, steady pace judgement, aerobic endurance
- 12–24 hours – mental strength, steady pace judgement, aerobic endurance
- team time trial – thorough warm-up, precision judgement to ride close behind the rider in front and change position smoothly and rapidly, careful pace judgment, aerobic effort on the cusp of the anaerobic threshold.

Starting out

Do not worry about your time when you take on time trialling initially – anything over 'evens' 32kmph (20mph) is considered respectable – whatever you record is a PB and you are bound to improve on your next attempt.

Short events

For short events – anything under an hour is short – the warm up is essential. Unless you ride out to the event, you should give yourself an hour's preparation time to sign on, collect your number, get changed into your racing clothes, use the toilet (there's often a queue), warm up and get to the start line.

Riders roll up to the timekeeper and wait for their number to be called. Ideally you should arrive with no more than a minute before your start time, breathing heavily and sweating lightly from your warm up, ready for action. Many riders queue up three or four minutes before their time – this is useful for later riders to judge their remaining warm-up time, but you are better off doing some light efforts up and down the road rather than standing astride your bike letting your muscles cool down. Just be careful – you can be disqualified from doing U-turns in the road within sight of the start.

You will be held up by a 'pusher' to start. This is your moment to compose yourself in readiness for the road ahead.

Make sure your chain is on the big chainring and one of the larger sprockets for your starting effort. You need to get up to speed quickly, but without over-cooking it. As you gain speed you can shift up a couple of gears and after two or three minutes you should be settled into your rhythm and pace for the event, tucked into a good aerodynamic position.

The key to successful time trialling is having an even output of effort over the whole distance of the event. If you have a heart rate monitor (HRM), you should aim to maintain a steady figure once you have settled down.

If you can, pick up the pace in the last couple of miles. You should cross the finish line exhausted, with no energy left.

Aerodynamic helmets are not essential when starting out, or at all unless you are looking at serious speeds.

Longer events

For 80–160km (50–100 mi.) events, you will need to pace yourself more carefully. You might be able to 'hang on' for the last kilometer or two in a 16 or a 40 but it's not so easy to do this in the last 10% of a 80 or 160 and still expect to have a reasonable time.

In terms of heart rate, riders will typically race 50s and 100s at five and ten beats per minute slower than their 25 pace. Of course, you may need to experiment with this. It's worth taking the first half of the event a little cautiously before stepping up the pace in the second half.

Endurance events

Rides lasting 12 and 24 hours are as much a mental challenge as a physical one. If you've done the training, you'll be prepared for the hours in the saddle and relishing the challenge ahead of you.

For a performance ride, you'll need helpers to hand up food and drink at appropriate times. But if you're seeking the ultimate test, you can ride these events unsupported.

The key to endurance events is maintaining a steady pace and not wasting any time along the way. Stops should be kept to a minimum, both in terms of their frequency and their duration. It's always best to ride within your limits in the first half of the event. Many riders set off at a pace they cannot sustain and then try to hang on for hours and hours. It's always a boost to be looking strong and catching others in the later stages – and it demoralises the opposition.

Beyond that, if you can press harder in the last hour (or half hour, or half a mile – whatever you can manage) you are almost bound to gain a few places on your rivals.

Pushing on

As you gain time trialling experience, you'll benefit from experimenting with your position – at least for the shorter distance events – tucking lower and narrower and being able to harness more muscular power. Perhaps more importantly, you'll develop a better sense of pacing yourself over the different distances and in varying conditions.

Interval training over very short distances is key to good time trialling. This will help to develop higher top speeds and so improve your overall average speeds. (For more information on interval training, see *Chapter 5*.)

Consider working with a coach to develop your time trialling skills, as a coach will help to manage your training, racing and resting time to make the most of the events you ride through the season.

HYDRATION

On events of 16km (25 mil.) or more, you'll need to take fluid on board. In most cases, one 500ml (1pt.) bottle should be sufficient for each hour. If you can, get a friend to hand up extra drinks in a 160km (100 mi.) trial – otherwise you'll have to manage with two 750ml (1.5pt.) bottles and hope that it's not too hot, or that the organisers are supplying drinks along the course.

HANDLEBAR POSITIONING

On anything over 160km (100 mi.), you'll find it more comfortable if you raise your handlebars by 2–3cm (0.8–1.1in.). On events of this length, comfort takes precedence over aerodynamics.

Mountain biking cross country

Like many of the cycling disciplines, cross country mountain biking is very easy to get into – there are races happening most weekends all across the country, most cycling shops organise weekly rides, and it is the perfect way to see more of the countryside.

Once you have been out on a few of these rides, and have honed your skills a little, it really is a pretty small step to get involved in a race. Nearly all races have a 'fun' category and this is designed precisely for people who want to try the sport out or who are most concerned with competing against themselves.

The main events
Cross country racing falls into three main categories:

1.   *Standard racing* – these are straightforward cross-country mountain bike races, where everyone makes a mad dash together in a mass start, invariably heading for a narrow gateway or single track before commencing numerous laps of a race that is likely to last between one and two hours. If you want to seriously compete in these events then you will need good off-road

Mountain biking is physically demanding, but the pain is outweighed by the fun and exhilaration.

technique, the ability to sprint, climb and descending, along with stamina and a basic understanding of mechanics for carrying out repairs.

2.   *Enduro events* – these races are more a test of stamina than a competition for first place. Events tend to be held over much larger circuits, often 50–100km (30–60 mi.) in challenging country. You need the same skills as for standard racing, but stamina and planning your fuelling strategy take on increased importance.

3.   *12–24 hour races* – these races embrace the two extremes. They are held over regular cross-country courses of about 10–20km (6–12 mi.) and are contested by solo riders, pairs or teams. As above, although you need plenty of mental strength and a sense of humour often helps you get through some difficult patches.

Starting out

As with most forms of racing, the best place to find a race is to ask at your local bike shop. Otherwise you can look up events on the internet or check the mountain biking magazines.

Just like the road and track events, allow yourself plenty of time to get registered and organised. Again, the shorter the event, the more important your warm up becomes. Mountain bike events often require riders to line up 10 minutes before the actual race time. This does nothing for your warm up – but at least everyone else has the same predicament. If you can, keep warm by moving about and wearing an extra layer of clothing.

The start of any mountain bike race is always hectic. Everyone sprints and jostles for position before the inevitable bottleneck. You can be the strongest rider on the course, but if you're stuck behind others on impassable sections of singletrack, you'll lose time to those riders ahead of you. That's why the start is absolutely crucial.

After a while, what tends to happen – in all mountain bike events – is that riders settle down to their own rhythm. Riders are strung out, almost as if they are riding a time trial. You'll probably find yourself in a tussle with one or two other riders of similar ability but on the whole you'll be riding at a pretty steady pace. However, it's wrong to think that mountain biking is all about a constant effort. Scientific evidence shows that mountain biking demands great fluctuations in power and effort. Climbs and rough ground demand great effort, whereas descents and technical sections may be tackled without any power at all – especially if you need to freewheel.

You don't have to have top notch technical skills to participate in a mountain bike event. No-one will worry if you need to get off your bike and push it over tricky sections. Of course, the more you practice off-road riding and racing, the more skilled and confident you'll become so you'll be able to ride more – and by default become a faster rider.

Mountain biking is definitely a matter of try it, you'll probably like it and have a lot of fun along the way.

Pushing on

With such an emphasis on technical skills, it is easy to get completely caught up with improving this aspect of riding if you want to improve cross country. However, it is well worth giving consideration to three other core skills:

- sprint
- cycling fitness
- maintenance.

The sprint is crucial if you are to push to the front at the start of a race – and once you have raced a couple of times you will appreciate this even more. If you don't get a quick start, you'll be making life difficult for yourself and playing catch-up for the rest of the race. Read the section on sprinting in *Chapter 2* (page 56) and, most importantly, get out and practice.

Don't get stuck in a rut of off-road riding – and we're not trying to subvert you to road racing! Without a doubt, you'll only develop your off-road skills by riding off road but you must also remember that it is an extremely physically taxing discipline. Most off-road specialists spend a great deal of time actually riding on the road. This is because you'll get far less of a pounding by riding on the road compared to off road and it's a great way to work on your speed.

Finally, it is well worth practising your maintenance and repair skills. The most likely mechanical problem you're going to encounter is a puncture. Barrie Clarke, the former Raleigh professional, was known for his ability to change the tube in his rear wheel and be back on his bike in under a minute. You don't get that good without practice (and a CO_2 pump).

Mountain biking downhill

Downhill mountain biking is probably closer to downhill skiing and track sprinting than it is to cross country mountain biking or any other cycling discipline. It's quick and it's exciting. You need nerves of steel, lightning reflexes and absolute determination to reach the bottom of the hill quicker than anyone else.

The main events

Due to the geography of Britain, there are not many long downhill events in the UK. The best tend to be found in Wales or Scotland. Depending where you live, it can be a long way to go for three or four minutes of competition (often less), but if that's your forte, that's what you'll have to do. (If you're good at downhilling, and nudging ever closer to the podium, then you probably won't mind travelling that much. Besides, it's no different from an athletics sprinter who may travel just for 10 seconds of competition.)

Some organisers like to offer an alternative competition – no chain downhilling. Your pedalling skills are out of the equation here – it's all about picking the best line, using your brakes as little as possible and adjusting your body position to the advantage of everything that gravity gives you. Totally insane and surprisingly popular.

Starting out

Prior to any downhill race the course should be mapped out so you can get an opportunity to study it beforehand. If you're lucky, it may even be marked with direction arrows along the way to help you negotiate the twists and turns. At the least, it will have two-tone tape defining the edge of the trail and marshals along the course to warn others of your breakneck descent.

Your course check is your chance to optimise your chances of success and to minimise the likelihood of something disastrous happening. Use the time to decide:
- what line to take
- what gears to select
- how hard your tyres and suspension should be
- when to change gear, brake, accelerate or jump.

For safety reasons, the course has to be marshalled, so your course inspection time will be limited. You may even be given time slots for when you can use the course. Make sure you make the most of it. Use the time to commit the course to memory by giving yourself some visual or mental cues so that you can flow into your next movement.

Sometimes practice times will be held on the day before the race (a bit like Formula 1 motor racing) and conditions can alter the course quite dramatically overnight. Heavy rain can turn solid ground into a quagmire, wind can bring a tree down. Even other riders practising after you can help to shift rocks or logs and change the ground surface with their wheels.

If you can, ask other riders what conditions are like. Most downhillers tend to treat the event like time triallists treat theirs – they'd love to win (or at least, do well) but accept that there are faster riders and they are quite happy just to post the best possible time they can manage. In fact, it's often quite easy to talk to other competitors, on the whole they are a pretty relaxed bunch – you will find yourself standing around together waiting for a lift back up to the top of the hill.

Pushing on

Go abroad – there is no substitute for foreign racing, either in Europe or the US, where the downhill courses are usually much longer and more demanding. Plus, of course, greater numbers of competitors tends to raise the competition bar. So if you can show well abroad you know you're doing the right things.

It's no coincidence that many of the top riders have moto-cross bikes. They don't necessarily race them, but riding moto-cross certainly helps to sharpen up the reflexes as everything happens that little bit quicker, and the bikes are even heavier so there is a training effect to handle the downhill bike.

DOWNHILL HELMETS

Downhilling is one of the few events cycling events where almost everyone wears a full-face helmet and protective body armour.

For novices, it's essential because of their lack of experience and skill. For experts, well, they'll be travelling at unbelievable speeds down some impossible slopes, so it makes sense to have protection in training and competition.

Cyclo-cross

Cyclo-cross is predominantly a winter sport. It's also probably the most accessible for anyone. The great thing about cross is that it takes place on a short circuit that can usually be lapped in under 10 minutes. It's good for spectators and it's encouraging for new riders. It doesn't matter if you're half the speed of the top riders, you can still participate and ride your own race.

Cross is also a great way to improve your bike handling skills – and that's useful for every discipline. Road riders will learn how to control their bikes in slippery conditions (useful if ever you have to go off-road to avoid a crash or obstacle in front of you!) and mountain bikers can benefit from the skills required to negotiate a (relatively) skinny-tyred bike off-road compared to blasting their way across the tracks on their usual fat-tyred, full-suspension bikes.

The main events

Cyclo-cross is a combination of off-road cycling and cross country running. When a rider encounters an obstacle that he can't ride, he leaps off his bike – shouldering it if necessary – and runs with it. Cyclo-cross races are short, no more than an hour (with the notable exception of the early season 60km (37mi.) Three Peaks race in Yorkshire which takes the winner close to three hours and the last finishers often twice that time). As a consequence, cross events tend to be fast.

The World Championships are held towards the end of January and the season tends to peter out after that. In the UK, there is a regional championship held in February, but, by this time, the non-specialist cross riders are usually seeking a little bit of a rest before moving on to preparation for a season of road or mountain bike racing.

Starting out

It's easy to begin racing cyclo-cross: find an event near your home (use the internet for the quickest search), turn up, pay your money, pin your number on your back, put your helmet on, line-up with your bike at the appropriate time, and follow everyone else. What could be simpler? It's a mad dash at the start as everyone jostles for position, but after the first lap the field tends to sort itself out and you can settle into your own rhythm. Don't be alarmed that some riders will be riding where you have to get off your bike and scramble over obstacles, or they can ride seemingly impossible gradients. This comes with practice.

As a novice you will find the stronger and more experienced riders lapping you. They will call out 'on your left' or 'on the right' expecting – quite rightly – you to move over to let them pass unhindered (to the right and left respectively in these two examples). Keep going until the judges call you to stop at the finish line. Riders' times are given as the time elapsed after the winner. For example, the winner might complete 9 laps in 1hr 8 min 12 sec. The next placed rider will be 'at 34 seconds' (or whatever) and so on, until we come to the lapped riders who are simply listed in order 'at 1 lap, at 2 laps, etc'.

Cross is excellent practice for all cyclists – it tests handling and builds fitness.

Cyclo-cross requires high levels of skill and stacks of practice, especially dismounting and remounting the bike. You also need to be able to run.

Cyclo-cross events are very sociable affairs. It helps that everything happens within a fairly small area and that spectators can frequently see the riders. Consequently, cyclo-cross events tend to be much more family-orientated than other cycling disciplines. Look around and note what equipment other riders are using. Ask them why they choose one component or frame over another. Most riders will be happy to share advice on equipment. For advice on your technique, you need to watch carefully what other riders are doing – even the juniors and younger riders can be a useful source of technique tips. Use them like a miner's canary – watch where they are falling over and treat the same area with caution. Note how the best riders tackle obstacles and turns – what's different about their approach compared to everyone else?

It certainly pays to reconnoitre the course beforehand. As long as you arrive early enough, there should be no problem in doing this – but don't do it when others are racing on the circuit. That's just not polite. A pre-race recce will help you identify the difficult places on the course, practise different racing lines and your run ups and shouldering the bike for different sections. This is an ideal time to get close and watch some of the top riders in action, too. Follow their lines and see how much faster you can go. Do be aware that the course can evolve during the course of a race. Logs or rocks can be kicked or moved out of place, and roots can become more slippery as the races (and warm ups) progress. So be prepared to amend your technique and racing lines as the event unfolds.

Pushing on

In really muddy conditions, the top riders have two or three spare bikes available and a helper to wash them down between each lap. This is an enormous asset, because in really poor conditions you can easily find that your bike has just about doubled in weight as mud collects around the front and rear brakes, the bottom bracket, rims and gears. Mud clogging the wheels and transmission will also make it difficult to ride and slow you down.

If you want to taste cyclo-cross at top level, go to Belgium. It is hugely popular there and you'll find a very cosmopolitan air about the events as Dutch, French and East European riders will also be present, making competition that much keener. If you're good, you'll probably find a local fan club springs up around you with willing helpers and fans to cheer you on at events.

WHAT TO RIDE

You can ride cyclo-cross on almost any bike, but something quite light, with fairly low gears, and reasonable clearance between the tyres and the frame (e.g. stripped down touring bike) is ideal. It's quite common for riders to post sales and wants at events, so keep your eyes open for second hand bargains.

Cyclo-sportive

Cyclo-sportive rides have been running on the Continent for years, but they've only recently caught the attention of the UK cycling media. The interest in these events has suddenly sky-rocketed, with manufacturers latching on and even marketing bikes and components specifically for sportive riders.

Sportives are simply challenge rides, usually held on the road (although some do have accompanying off-road events). They attract a wide range of participants: from keen club riders eager to test themselves to top racers using the events as training races, alongside others challenging their own limits of endurance whilst some are just happy to be there. Many events cater for a wide audience by offering three or four courses with different levels of difficulty (largely dictated by length).

The main events

The sportive calendar is growing all the time. Some sportives have been established for years running in tandem with the road race Classics (e.g. Paris-Roubaix), while others have grown up a sportives in their own right (e.g. La Marmotte). One of the most recent additions to the sportive calendar is the Etape du Tour – a stage in the Tour de France for amateur riders, held on the day before the race itself follows the exact same roads. Thousands of riders, the race banners, barriers, and gendarmes creates an amazing buzz and makes the Etape a really memorable experience.

Starting out

Most sportives are long, somewhere in the region of 150–250km (90–160 mi.) and invariably they involve at least one significant climb.

To deal with this, you need to make sure you have plenty of kilometres under your wheels and have been tackling the longest hills you can find in your area. Long club rides should help to build up your stamina and riding with others will make the time pass more easily. If you are new to cycling, you are bound to pick up some very useful tips by riding with more experienced cyclists. To really get the necessary distance done in training, audax rides of 200–300km (125–190 mi.) are excellent preparation.

Although sportives are largely informal rides, their popularity means that you will have to enter in advance. However, even for those events abroad, this should not pose too much of a problem as most now have websites and the key information is often in English (or simple enough to understand) and payments can often be made by credit card. The entry fee may include a 'free' jersey or other souvenir items (to be collected at registration, on the day or day before the event) and loan of a timing chip (fitted to your frame or forks). For some events, the organisers ask that you do wear the event jersey on the ride – the sight of thousands of riders all in matching jerseys is quite something!

Some of the larger events have now grown so big that foreign entries are often handled by a small number of selected agents in different countries. For many riders, this makes life a great deal more simple as the agents deal with everything – arranging transport for you and your bike and accommodation – and guide you through the maze of halls, stalls, tents and desks that make up the registration and start area. Not only does this take a great deal of stress out of the event, but it means that if you want it, you'll have some company on the ride and plenty of new friends to share your experiences with over a beer or two after the ride.

On the other hand, if you are comfortable with the language and nuances of the event you may feel constrained by having to compromise for the needs of the group. Apart from looking for another event, there's not much you can do if the organisers go down this route to simplify their administration.

Cyclo-sportive events are great way of experiencing new surroundings.

Be aware that sportives do have time limits. You can't take forever to ride one – or you will find the timing equipment at the finish has been packed up and your ride will not be validated. Or worse, you will be pulled out of the event somewhere along the route and will have to spend the rest of the day sitting in the 'sag wagon' creeping behind the last rider waiting for them to crack.

Pushing on

If you are really keen and want to take the challenge more seriously, you can work your way to the head of the field and duke it out with the big hitters. The bigger Continental sportive rides carry a great deal of prestige, and an excellent prize list. Just be prepared for full-on racing. The top sportive riders are likely to have helpers along the route and team tactics will be employed to get the edge over their rivals.

It does seem a little incongruous that these rides have a winner – but that's the great attraction about them, you can ride them at any level you want. You can race against some tough opposition in more challenging circumstances than your local road race league. You can test yourself to achieve a gold, silver or bronze standard time (set by the organisers). Or you can saunter round as part of an amazing cycling spectacle, following an awesome route in some great company and every bystander cheering you on.

Developing
training plans

Introduction

The final piece in the jigsaw, to see yourself as the cycling maestro that you have always dreamed of becoming, is to do the training. This chapter brings together the races or riding that you plan to do, with the skills and physical capabilities that you need to perform, into a single, structured programme of training.

We'll start by asking you a few probing questions so that you can take an honest look at your riding ambitions and your day-to-day life. For a start, are they compatible? The next step is to put some realistic goals in place so that you can monitor your progress and give yourself that all-important pat on the back every once in a while. We'll then look at the key types of training that you can use to improve every aspect of your cycling. Then, and only then, we will let you loose on the training programmes.

Self-assessment

Before you find a copy of the training plan used by Chris Boardman, Lance Armstrong, Sven Nijs or Bart Brentjens and start following it religiously, you need to check your own situation. It's no good trying to follow the plan of a top pro if you're holding down a full-time job and actually you just want to ride local 10 and 25mi. time trials. Their training is based on years of foundation training and racing – they are paid to ride their bikes *and* rest in order that they are ready for competition against the best in the world.

There are two good methods for taking a look at yourself: lifestyle analysis and SWOT analysis. They are not mutually exclusive, and there's no harm in running yourself through both tests.

Lifestyle analysis

Before you can put any meaningful programme of training together, you need to establish where you are now, what's brought you here, and where you want to reach. You also need to understand how much time and commitment you can give to your cycling. If you work full-time and have a young family, you probably won't be able to dedicate as much time to training as someone who is single and working part-time. (That's not to say your training can't be smarter and produce better results than the almost full-time bike rider.)

Take a pen and a piece a paper and answer the following questions – and be truthful with yourself.

- What cycling experience do you have and what are your best achievements?
- What road, track or MTB category are you?
- What were your best two performances last season, and why?
- What are your strengths?
- What are your weaknesses?
- How much time do you have to train each week?

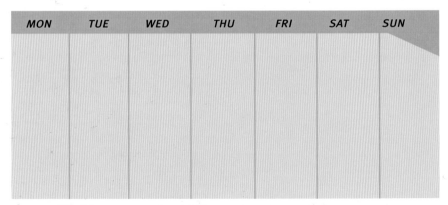

	MON	TUE	WED	THU	FRI	SAT	SUN
MORNING							
AFTERNOON							
EVENING							

- What training are you doing at the moment?

MON	TUE	WED	THU	FRI	SAT	SUN

- What is your current weight?
- If you have been tested, what is your maximum power output?
- What is your maximum heart rate?
- What is your resting heart rate?
- What do you want to achieve in the next season?
- What do you want to achieve in the next three years?

No doubt you will already know the answers to all – or most – of these questions, but by committing them to paper it often helps you be a lot more realistic in establishing where you are now and, therefore, where you can realistically aim to get to.

SWOT analysis

If you work in business, you'll be familiar with this form of analysis. SWOT stands for:

- Strengths
- Weaknesses
- Opportunities
- Threats.

A daily commute is often the best time to train, so structure your training week around this.

Strengths

Write down your strengths – what you're good at: is it your sprint, your climbing ability, how you read a race or perhaps the ability to train hard?

Your strengths can serve either to select those events where you will excel, or you can use this as a reminder not to spend so much time on this aspect of your riding. If you're a good climber, you might want to ride hilly events. But instead of trying to be an even better climber, why not improve your downhill skills (it's surprising how often good climbing and poor descending and vice versa go together)? By stopping to think what you're not so good at, you've just identified another opportunity – something to work on to make you a better bike rider.

Weaknesses

Next, write down your weaknesses. This might include the mad dash at the start of a mountain bike race, cornering off-camber, riding in a bunch or getting out of bed to go training. Again, the list might put you off some types of event – for example, if you're poor at accelerating you may wish to avoid road and track races, and stick to time trials. On the other hand, if you know you're strong, work on your change of pace and you could do well in bunch races. Even within a preferred discipline most riders can identify something that lets them down.

Opportunities

Within opportunities, include the events that you could ride (obviously some you can't because of entry restrictions on licence, age or gender, or calendar clashes with other races or activities) and when, how and where you can train.

It's surprising what's around if you look. There are often unadvertised local time trials, league races or informal training groups. Local bike shops, other riders and coaches are a rich source of information. Consider other disciplines too. If you're a road rider, why not give track racing or mountain biking a go? You never know, you might find you do really well and enjoy it.

Threats

Finally, threats – this covers anything that could possibly stop you. Maybe you want to race abroad but you don't have a passport or letter of authority. Perhaps you're doing shift work and that interferes with your training and racing schedule. You really ought to spend some time with your partner or family. Can you finance your cycling? There could be a whole host of things threatening your path to cycling utopia, but only you can identify them all.

When you know what the threats are, you can do something about them. Apply for your passport now, speak to your boss about a possible change in your work schedule, make a deal with your partner or family so that they get to see you wearing something other than Lycra and not only when you are totally exhausted after a long training bash or race.

It's a simple exercise but worth doing, as it often brings up some surprises either as problems or solutions.

Using a coach

It is well worth considering using the services of a coach before you embark on developing your own training plan. The coach will often ask you many more questions than listed here – particularly covering your medical history. They will also be more objective and realistic – probing certain answers to get to the root of issues and helping you to set your own challenges and achievable targets.

Before you pick up the phone or sign your life savings away to an unknown name on a list, consider a few questions to pose to your potential new best friend (and secret weapon):

A coach will be able to make sense of your analysis, ensuring that you balance training, family and work commitments.

QUESTION	WHAT YOU NEED TO KNOW
What coaching qualifications do you have?	Coaches should have a valid and recognised coaching qualification from their governing body. This should include insurance cover, but also establish to what level and in which environments or disciplines they are qualified to coach.
What experience do you have of coaching in my cycling discipline (or with riders of my ability, age or gender)?	A good coach should be able to apply themselves to any rider's needs but it makes sense for your coach to have some experience or interest (either as a rider or as a coach) in your chosen area, with riders similar to yourself, particularly if you need technical help. Many coaches never see their riders on a bike but successfully use e-mail and telephone to communicate with them. You may be able to pick up technical skills elsewhere and use your coach to help with your conditioning, planning your season and race strategies, and analysing your results or weaknesses.
To what level have you coached riders before?	Find out what success your coach has had with other riders. If possible, speak to those riders and discover what they liked or disliked about the coach and his or her methods.
How much time would you give to me?	Be realistic. Unless you are paying them a full-time wage, you cannot expect them to devote 24 hours a day to your needs. For most riders, 1–3 hours a week should be ample time to discuss progress and allow time for the coach to prepare your training programme and analyse your performance.
What happens if I'm ill or injured?	You may be able to negotiate a reduced fee or extend your contract but don't expect your money back just because you're not training or racing. A good coach should still take an interest in the rider's health and help them back to form during the recovery and rehabilitation period.

QUESTION	WHAT YOU NEED TO KNOW
What can you do for me?	Decide what you think you need and ask the coach what services he or she offers. Is it hands-on technique training (which may be difficult for endurance disciplines), time and lifestyle management, programme planning, laboratory or field tests, nutrition advice, bike set-up, or video analysis? You many not need all or any of these aspects but listen to what the coach can do and establish what he or she will provide.
When can I contact you?	Your coach may look after other riders and have other commitments, so you need to agree when, and how frequently, it is convenient for you to contact him or her.
What do you need from me?	Before you get anything from your coach, expect the coach to ask you a lot of questions to establish what you are doing now and what you wish to achieve. Coaches need feedback. Most will provide forms for you to record your training and racing results. Make sure you can give this feedback. Walk away if the coach offers you a 'standard programme', doesn't ask for at least monthly feedback or if you feel the coach doesn't want enough from you!
Can we meet?	It's a good idea to meet your coach – preferably before you part with any money – and to help establish some rapport. Some coaches may offer an initial 'interview' session, either free or for a one-off fee, for you to decide if you want to work together. After that, it's up to you to decide together how frequently (if at all) you need to meet.
How much do you charge?	There is no regulation of coaching fees. You have to decide whether the coach's fee is reasonable or not. You might compare figures with those of gym membership, personal trainers, coaches in other sports or even private tutors in languages or music. After all, you're paying for someone's time and expertise to help you improve a skill.
If I decide this is not for me, how much notice do I need to give you?	Do allow time for the coach's methods to bear fruit but find out if you can terminate the relationship at any time. It's not unreasonable for a coach to stipulate that you sign up for a minimum of three months and give at least one month's notice if you don't intend to continue.
Will you make me into a champion?	If the coach promises you 'yes', he or she is lying and you're deluding yourself! The coach can help you, but you have to do the hard work, the training and racing, and have the motivation to succeed.

Training records are important tools to assess your performances. They can provide a template with which to repeat a similar training pattern and produce good results again. They can also be used to identify reasons behind poor results so that remedial action can be taken and disappointing performances can be avoided in the future. By using a training diary you can monitor your progress, recording the duration, intensity and frequency of your cycling activities.

You can record as much or as little as you like in your training diary and it can take any form you like – ranging from an old notebook that just records the hours on the saddle and distances covered to a complex spreadsheet which gives all manner of fancy graphs and covering heart rates, body weight, training variables.

Try to record the daily values of your resting heart rate, hours and quality of sleep, and subjective 'feel-good' ratings – both generally – and in training or racing. Check your weight every 1-4 weeks too. Like HR, your weight needs to be recorded at a regular time of day, i.e. first thing in the morning or last thing at night.

Trends in any and all of this data will be a sure sign that you are doing something right (or wrong). Keeping a training diary also acts as a good early warning system – if your resting heart rate spikes upwards, there is a good chance you are overdoing the training, so take it easy for a few days to prevent an injury or illness.

Goal-setting

Years ago, the pro riders would ride everything – early season races before the classics in the spring, followed by a series of small stage races prior to the really big events like the three-week Giro d'Italia or Tour de France in mid-summer. This was followed by post-Tour criteriums, the autumn classics and World Championships. The last riders to have successful 'all-round' seasons were the likes of Bernard Hinault and Sean Kelly in the 1980s. In the mid-1980s, American rider Greg Lemond brought a whole new focus to the Tour de France, winning it in 1986, 1989 and 1990. Since Lemond, we have seen first Miguel Indurain and then Lance Armstrong dominate Le Tour by setting this as their sole aim for the year to the exclusion of everything else. These are prime examples of goal-setting at the highest level.

Goal-setting helps you to focus on particular targets and split a daunting task into manageable stepping stones. It is a useful technique to aid motivation. It can help you justify the time spent training, riding in the rain, sticking to a particular diet or making personal sacrifices either preparing for or actually executing your personal mission. You don't have to start every race expecting to win it – that's almost certainly heading for a fall – but you can set yourself minor 'process goals' to achieve in all of your races and even training sessions. Such process goals might be: to stay in the bunch in the first half of the race, to cover all attacks in the second half of the race, to improve your pedalling technique by not using the big chainring, or to make sure you drink at least 500ml every hour.

With well-defined goals, it's a simple matter to see whether or not you have achieved your goal for each particular race or training session.

Mental preparation is the key to high level performance – be focussed.

I'll prepare to be on form for one event a year. A maximum of two peaks. Never more.

Victoria Pendleton, World and Commonwealth sprint champion

SMARTER training

Another technique adapted from the business world is that of using SMARTER targets:

- *Specific* – you need to focus on a particular target, event, time or achievement, not a generic aim such as 'to do better'.

- *Measurable* – goals need to be measurable: so that you know when you have reached your objective time it will take to ride a certain distance, or have a target distance or event to aim for.

- *Agreed* – share your goal with someone else. Family members are more likely to provide help and support if you tell them what you are doing so they can understand why you are spending time on your bike or abstaining from certain foods. Agreeing your goals with a coach will allow him or her to tailor your training programme, working on your strengths and weaknesses and ensuring that you reach peak fitness at the right time. Plus, it is more difficult to back away from your goal if you have shared it with someone else!

- *Realistic* – be sensible. Set yourself a challenge, but if you are over 40 you are unlikely to get a professional contract to compete in the Tour de France, or if your time is limited by work or family commitments you are not going to be able to spend six months touring around South America (at least, not for a while).

- *Time phased* – decide when you are going to achieve your goal. This year, next year, within the five years? Without a definite time scale it is too easy to put the goal off time and time again and never actually do it.

- *Exciting* – if your goal does not excite you, then it will be extremely difficult to motivate yourself to achieve it. Goals should really stretch you and give you satisfaction when completed. *You* have to decide on your goal. It is not something that can be decided for you.

- *Recorded* – write down your goal. Use a diary, or leave a note by the bathroom mirror or next to your bike to remind you what you are aiming for.

Look at the following goal-setting statements:
- to be fitter
- to be a better bike rider
- to be a better climber.

The list looks admirable, but they all miss out on at least one of the criteria above. As a result, they are impossible to monitor and there is no end point to them.

But with a bit of thought and structure, it is easy to develop SMARTER goals such as:
- to ride a sub-24.00 minute 10mi. time trial this season
- to gain 30 points on my road-racing licence by the end of June
- to climb my local off-road hill in the big chainring by the end of next month.

Milestones

When dealing with goals set over large periods of time – say, a racing season – you need to set a series of milestones. Tackling the one major goal will be very difficult to monitor and levels of motivation will invariably fall away.

Start with your major goal and work backwards – look at the time you have available and calculate the rate of progression you will need to accomplish the task. You can then break this down into manageable steps to get from where you are now to where you want to be in, say, six months' time. Think of it as looking at map of where you want to go, and deciding the route and speed of your journey.

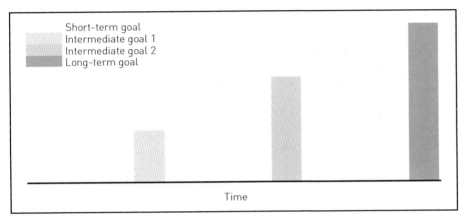

Short-term goal
Intermediate goal 1
Intermediate goal 2
Long-term goal

Time

Smart training needs to take you out of your comfort zone occasionally.

TRAINING DEVICES – HEART RATE MONITORS

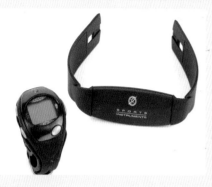

Heart-rate monitors (HRMs) quantify intensity of exercise and, if used correctly, are extremely useful tools. They range in complexity from basic models which simply tell you your current heart rate to those which can download data to a computer and produce a vast array of tables and charts.

Your heart rate is a good marker for the intensity of effort during exercise – as effort increases, your heart rate increases. HRMs provide an objective figure to quantify your training. Speed alone can be deceptive. You could easily ride at 40kph or 50kph – downhill, or with a tailwind, or in bunch behind other riders. But you have not ridden hard to achieve that speed. On the other hand, covering 30km in two hours may not look impressive – but up a mountain or into the teeth of a gale you will have worked much harder than the figures suggest. An HRM will see beyond these situations to the actual effort you put in.

Maximum heart rate

Most training scales are based on percentages of a rider's maximum heart rate (MHR). The only true way to find this is by an exhaustive test on an ergometer under supervised conditions – however, this is expensive, difficult to achieve and physically very unpleasant. As a result, a number of formulae have been developed to find your MHR – these should be used with caution as they can give variable results. It is a question of using the test and finding how the results work for you.

A simple rule of thumb to calculate MHR is: 220 – age (e.g. a 23 year-old's maximum heart will be 220–23 = 197). This is an approximate figure and individuals will differ, but it will give a rough guideline suitable for many people.

This is what too much Zone 6 training does to you...

The next stage is to calculate your maximum working heart rate – not to be confused with maximum heart rate. To do this:

1. Find your resting heart rate – this is best done by taking a pulse within ten minutes of waking up in the morning, preferably while still laying down. It is also best to take readings over a period of a week and use an average result.
2. Then subtract your resting heart rate from your MHR. For example, if our 23-year-old cyclist has a resting heat rate of 58, this gives him a working heart rate of 139.

Finally, you take whatever percentage of working heart rate that you are aiming for (e.g. 75% would be 139 x 0.75 = 104) and add this to your resting heart rate (e.g. 104 + 58 = 162). This gives you the target heart rate that you should aim for.

How many Zones?

Peter Keen, the sports scientist and later Performance Director for British Cycling, identified and developed a system of training zones for cycling training – it comprises six Zones of Training plus a Recovery Zone. There are other zone methods but Keen's is well established and forms the basis of the programmes in this book. You will note in the table below that these levels correspond to Borg's rate of perceived exertion (RPE) that we looked at in Chapter 3 (page 85).

Training band or Zone	Recovery	Basic		Intensive		Maximal	
		Zone 1	Zone 2	Zone 3	Zone 4	Zone 5	Zone 6
% MHR	< 60	60–65	65–75	75–82	82–89	89–94	94+
RPE (see page 85)	1	2	3	5	6	7	10
Durarion of a continious training session	< 60mins	1.5–6.0hours	1–4hours	45–120mins	30–60mins	15–40mins	4–10mins OR intervals
Sensation	Easy, apparently effortless	Easy breathing. Able to hold a conversation when riding	Breathing generally easy, a little deeper on hills	More concentration. Breathing heavier	Conversation reduced to simple sentences	Deep breathing. Brief words only	Lung-busting. Can utter no more than a weight-lifter's grunt!
Pace	Very easy	Easy	Brisk	Fast	Racing	Sprinting	Flat out
Fitness component developed	Recovery	Aerobic endurance and Strength			Muscular speed, Muscle power and Short-term muscle endurance		

Long, steady distance can mean hours riding alone – so build in a group ride to keep sharp and motivated.

Training sessions

There are a range of sessions that you can introduce to your training programme in order to ensure variety – which will help your motivation – and to hone the specific skills and attributes that you will need to ride in your chosen discipline.

Warm-up

Warm-up helps to prepare you for exercise. It raises your heart rate and body temperature, preparing your muscles for the effort to follow, and can be used to focus your mind to the task in hand. The shorter the effort, the greater the need for the warm-up. It's common to see riders at international track meetings riding on the rollers for 45 minutes or more prior to their event, whereas cyclo-sportive riders are usually quite happy to roll up to the start line and ride (although if you're wanting to ride with the leading riders, a good warm-up is well advised, as the head of the field in such events can be every bit as tough as any road race).

It is worth spending at least the first ten minutes of any session warming up – your body will be prepared for the effort to follow, and you greatly reduce the likelihood of picking up muscle strains and other similar injuries, plus it is an ideal opportunity to prepare yourself mentally for the exercise you are about to undertake.

Long, steady distance

Regardless of which discipline you are riding, these rides are likely to form the foundation of your training. There's no getting away from the fact that you need a good base mileage. Unless you are a cyclo-cross rider, much of this will be done in the winter and early spring. Speed will not be excessive (indeed, some coaches call the phase long, *slow* distance).

If you are new to cycling, build up with progressively longer rides. This will help to get your muscles (and backside) used to cycling, recruiting more 'Type 1' slow-twitch muscle fibres and adapting to fat-burning as an alternative fuel for energy. Trained cyclists are much more efficient at fat burning, which allows them to sustain their effort for longer and with less fatigue. In addition, your body will increase the number of mitochondria (subcellular muscle structures that produce aerobic energy) and increase the density of capillaries to carry more oxygen to the muscles.

Intervals

These are one of the most effective sessions that you can use to improve your speed. In their simplest form intervals are short, repeated, very intense efforts interspersed by periods of lower intensity.

There are different interpretations of interval training. Most interval programmes use the same time for the effort as the recovery. For example, you might do six repetitions of two minutes at Zone 5 with two minutes recovery in between each one. However, the times can be stretched either way for proportionately longer effort to rest ratios, or vice versa. For example, you could do an 8–second Zone 6 sprint every minute for 6 minutes, with 52 seconds, recovery between each one – or perhaps you could do 6 x 60 seconds at Zone 5 with 2–3 minutes' rest between each one.

Interval training is an ideal tool to increase a rider's overall speed. You can initially break down a 4,000m pursuit or a 25–mile time trial into smaller sections by covering 4 x 1,000m, or two sets of 5 x 2.5-mi. at close to race pace. As you gain fitness and your speed increases with your training, you can increase the length of the efforts and decrease the rest periods in between.

However, interval training is very exhausting and is best limited to no more than a couple of sessions a week.

Fartlek

Fartlek translates as 'speedplay' and is a Scandinavian running technique, developed in the 1960s, in which a group would be running together at a comfortable pace and one of them would attack, perhaps for 100m at high speed or maybe for 500m somewhere above the group's pace, and the group would have to change their pace to match that of the leader.

You can do just the same in a cycling group, simulating attacks in an on-road or off-road race. Do look behind and make sure it is safe to move first!

Even if you're not in a group it's possible to have these varying distance and intensity efforts. For example, each time you see a white car, sprint at Zone 6 for 100m and each time you see a red car, go hard at Zone 4 until you pass the next street sign. You make this more difficult by having each car 'trump' the other.

If you live close to an urban area this could certainly provide you with a good-quality workout! Make it a little easier on yourself by going with every fifth or sixth white or red car, or specifying a make and model.

Off-road you can choose different markers, such as gateposts, rocks or particular species of trees, but the principles are the same.

Fartlek training can form a good part of group training – it also makes training fun.

TRAINING DEVICES – TURBO TRAINERS

Bad weather and dark evenings can be overcome by a good session indoors on a turbo trainer. The basic idea of the turbo trainer is to provide a stationary support via a folding 'A' frame. The bike's rear wheel is then clamped (over the quick release lever) into the frame and a roller is usually pressed up against the rear tyre. This roller has a heavy flywheel attached to it on one end and a resistance unit (air fan, oil fan or magnetic resistance unit depending on how much noise you want to make and how much money you have to spend – the higher the price, the lower the noise) on the other end.

The turbo trainer is ideal for high quality 20–60 minute work outs, raising your heart-rate to higher levels for fitness gains and to develop cycling-specific muscle. Do not attempt to replicate a long ride on a turbo-trainer – you will become very numb and very bored. Concentrate on good quality exercise – most of your sessions will be in Zones 3 to 6. Wipe the bike down when you've completed your session, have a shower and then relax or do whatever you need to do in your daily life.

A conservatory, garage, cellar or garden shed are all good places to set up the indoor cycling studio – mainly because you get very hot very quickly, but also because turbo trainers are quite noisy. Ventilation is essential for your comfort, and although it may be cold in the garage you will be sweating and spluttering in no time, so it will be a comfortable temperature after a few minutes.

Here are some top tips for using a turbo trainer:
- Allow at least 10 minutes to warm up and cool down, using low gears
- Have a plan for each session, make them progressive and include variety – mix in short sprints, long sprints, sustained efforts, progressive exercises, one-legged pedalling, intervals, etc.
- Buy a floor standing office fan (otherwise you will get very hot after just a few minutes)
- Cover the floor under the bike and trainer – a rubber mat will help dampen the vibrations and it will also prevent sweat dripping on the floor coverings
- Cover your bike – a towel over the handlebars will do the trick. Sweat is salty and plays havoc with your paint work and expensive components, another reason to have a 'turbo specific' bike
- Have a towel handy to wipe your face too
- Have a big drink ready for during the workout and after, you will sweat at an alarming rate and therefore dehydrate very quickly
- Place a mirror in front of the turbo so you can keep an eye on your technique (or just admire yourself, if you're vain!)
- Make a few 30-45 minute playlists of motivational music to listen to
- Make videos or DVDs of motivational bike races to watch while you ride.

Pyramids

These are progressively harder efforts, until you reach a peak, and then come down the other side with the same pattern. The aim of this session is to raise your lactate threshold, enhance your ability to recover and improve your speed.

For example:

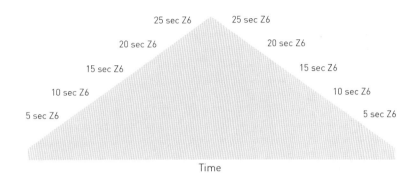

Reverse pyramids

Sometimes it's worth employing a reverse pyramid – in order to increase the time you spend in the maximal training zones. Here, after a good warm-up, you do the longest effort first and then do progressively shorter efforts before increasing the length of effort again.

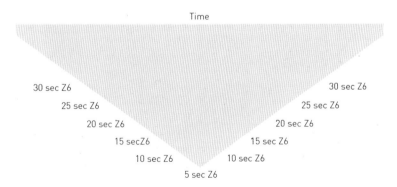

Variations

Of course, you don't have to 'go up and down' the pyramid with just one effort at each level or duration of intensity. You could do two or three efforts of each duration before moving onto the next, or you could string big blocks of effort together. For example, you could do 6 x 5-second Zone 6 efforts, take a short rest and then 6 x 10-second Zone 6 efforts, followed by a short rest and 6 x 15-second efforts until you reach your chosen peak and then start to descend the pyramid once again.

Alternatively, you can adjust the volume of efforts you do (the advantage here is that you can better maintain the quality of your effort throughout the session):

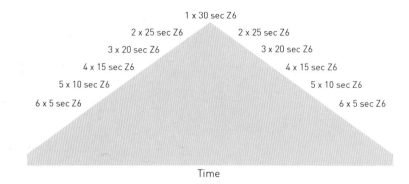

Or adjust the volume and intensity of the efforts:

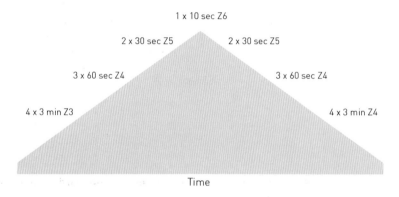

Extended sprints and power sprints are the finishing touch and need to build on solid base training.

Leg speed intervals

Leg speed intervals are best executed in a moderate gear and will improve your lactate threshold, cadence and ability to repeat high-speed efforts. Accelerate in the saddle and maintain a high cadence – around 120–130rpm – for a minute before recovering for a minute. Repeat the pattern for 20 minutes. You can achieve even greater leg speeds by pedalling downhill or with a tailwind.

Extended sprints

As the name suggests, these are long sprints to develop your peak speed and acceleration. You can do these on any training ride. Simply accelerate out of the saddle, and as you reach your peak speed sit down and maintain this pace for another 10–20 seconds. As you get fitter, increase the duration of the effort. Top riders aim to maintain their speed for up to 5 minutes.

Power sprints

These sprints aim to produce explosive speed as needed for any sprint situation, attacking in road races, and the start of mountain bike and cyclo-cross races. Find a quiet, flat stretch of road or trail, and after a good warm-up roll almost to a halt. In a big gear, accelerate as hard as you can for 10–15 seconds. Allow yourself time to recover and repeat this 6–8 times. Add resistance by riding slightly uphill or into the wind, or using a bigger gear.

Tapering and peaking

It is simply not possible to continue improving your strength, speed and general fitness at a steady rate. Initially you can make greater gains, but your rate of improvement will diminish as you become fitter, and if you train too much you will become tired and over-trained. In order to 'peak' (be at your best possible form) for an important event, you need to taper your training. The greater the demands of the forthcoming event, the more tapering you will need to do, but the usual period is around 5–21 days.

For example, in the three weeks prior to a 12-hour time trial you might race 100mi., 50mi. and 25mi. This will ensure that you are not too fatigued before the 12-hour race and the shorter events will help to develop some extra speed.

Riders tackling the long endurance events like the Tour de France or Race Across America often aim to arrive at the race just slightly under-trained. If they begin the race in absolute peak form they can only tire in the subsequent days and weeks. By having the capacity to handle more work, they not only improve their chances of surviving the duration of the whole race, but the psychological boost of getting stronger as the race continues and other riders begin to fade is an enormous benefit too.

Weights and gym work

Specificity would encourage you to become a better bike rider by simply riding a bike more. However, sometimes this is not the perfect answer and it pays to look at other ways to improve your performance. Using weights and gym work are an ideal example.

The big advantage of sessions in a gym is that you can work on individual muscle groups. For example, there is relatively little you can do to improve your upper body strength on the bike, but it's an easy matter to do some exercises or lift some weights to isolate this area and make some significant improvements. Track sprinters and mountain bikers in particular can benefit from weight training to improve their riding abilities, but road and time trial riders may also wish to develop core stability and improve strength in their backs.

As a cyclist, you don't want to develop big muscles, these will simply weigh you down and reduce your range of movement – just look at how a body builder walks and you'll see what we mean! Instead, you want gains in strength without the increase in muscle bulk. To do this, you need to do weight training (as opposed to weight lifting). This involves lifting relatively low weights a high number of times.

Just like working to Zones of Training, you can use the same method to calculate your training weights. Go to a gym – you'll have to have a safety induction to show you how to use the equipment – and speak to one of the trainers, explaining what you want and why. They will be able to help you with a progressive programme to develop your strength, focussing on particular machines or styles of lifting free weights. You need to find the maximum weight you can lift by making small incremental increases in the weights used without going to the point of exhaustion or straining yourself! When you find a weight that is tiring to lift three times, use that as your maximum. For your training purposes, you can then use 50–75% of this value.

Cross train a lot. It addresses muscle imbalance, core strength and ligament and connective tissue strength – all things that can prevent injury during crashes and also prevent overuse injuries caused by poor technique and posture. And pay close attention to flexibility work.

Jenny Copnall, multi-national Cross Country Champion and National Points Champion

Each lift is a repetition (or 'rep') and a group of reps is a 'set'. You can then organise your training into sets. For example, you might do 3 sets of 12 bench presses at 60% of your maximum, with a short rest interval between each set.

- Lift and lower the weight slowly – typically on a 'two-three' count (lift the weight to the count of two, lower to the count of three)
- Make sure you lift and lower over the whole range of movement, otherwise you will lose flexibility
- Alternate muscle groups from one exercise to the next – for example, chest then back; biceps then triceps
- Always focus on the using the correct technique – remember quality not quantity. Not only will this help you to avoid injury, it will also deliver better results
- Keep hydrated during the session, just as you would out on your bike.
- Do not attempt to lift more than you can cope with. Weight training should not be competitive. Showing off is the quickest route to an injury
- Have a towel with you. Wipe equipment before and after use
- Record your sessions in a notebook or on a chart after each exercise, so that you build up progressively and have rest weeks (just like your riding programme)

Vary your trainig to include gym work and running – you'll feel the benefits and the change will help motivation.

An hour or two each week, especially during the winter, will do wonders for your strength in readiness for the next season. Reduce the time spent in the gym when the riding season begins.

You can also use the gym for circuit training, mixing exercises such as press-ups, squat jumps, steps and sit-ups, with brief periods on the free weights or machines. Many gyms run these sessions for groups and they are great for motivation, as you have to move on from one exercise to the next with little time to rest in between each one.

TRAINING DEVICES – CYCLING COMPUTERS

Even a very basic cycling computer will have average speed and distance functions. Average speed is the easiest training device to use in training – it's especially useful when comparing time trial times and previous performance on a set course or regular training route.

Cadence is perhaps the most beneficial function of the cycle computer – it allows riders to use cadence drills and help select the right gearing for time trial efforts, or to help maintain consistent pedalling during training. See *Chapter Two* (page xx) for more on pedalling and cadence).

As with all data that relates to your cycling, keep it in your training diary and you will find many ways to use it to gauge your performance.

Ready-made training programmes

Sitting down with a completely blank piece of paper to draw up your own training programme can be daunting, so we have put together a number of generic training programmes to get you going.

These programmes do not cover every event, discipline or distance – they offer a broad selection to give you an idea of the goals that you should be aiming for in your training. You can follow the programmes as they are or you can use them as a framework for creating a programme tailored to your needs.

Road Racing

Road racing offers arguably the greatest scope of race distances of any cycling discipline – it would be easy to fill the chapter with programmes just for the road. However, the basic components will be the same regardless of the race – you just need to make alterations to the riding times and intensity levels. For example, if you're going to specialise in town centre criteriums, there's little point in spending hours on the bike with long-distance endurance training. Your needs are going to be closer to those of the track specialists, with shorter, faster, more intense efforts. Of course, if you intend to ride Premier Calendar races or stage races, then you'll need a much better endurance foundation and a greater variety of skills to cope with a wider range of terrain.

It's always nice to train in the sunshine if you can manage it.

80km Road Race

Riding 80km (50mi.) at a race pace is quite different from 'just riding' this distance – you will be looking at completing the distance in about two hours as a 2nd or even 3rd category rider. Fourth category riders may take an extra 5–10 minutes to complete the distance. In a really quick race, elite riders may complete the distance at nearly 50kph (30mph), resulting in a race time of about 1 hour 40 minutes. That means that the race is going to be fairly brisk and, at times, will take you out of your comfort zone. This is most likely to happen when the 'hammer comes down' and you are called upon to sprint, either to make a charge or to close on other riders who try and get away. In order to be prepared for this you need to have good base fitness so that you have energy in the tank when you need to make these extra efforts and you need power in your legs to deliver the bursts of speed.

If possible, the best way to train for road races is in a group or chaingang. Not only will this get you used to riding in close proximity of other bikes, but it will also help to share the effort.

Assuming that you have kept a basic level of winter training, and the miles have been ticking over, you could use the following programme for an early season event (this would fall in the transition phase of your season cycle).

Variations

- In mid-season you may be racing once, twice or three times a week, in which case you need to spend more time resting and less time training – as each race actually becomes training for the next event
- Analyse each race to identify your weaknesses and amend your training accordingly – but be careful, unless you have a balanced approach, this can easily lead to over-training
- Those riders competing in longer events or stage races should have at least one ride a week of at least 3–4 hours, but use other training sessions to hone their speedwork
- If you're coming back from injury or illness, reduce the training schedule or intensity to 50%of normal. Then increase the volume or intensity by 10–20% over the next 2–3 weeks until you're back on track.

Keep your upper body still. You've got to relax and keep your pedalling smooth – that way you'll be efficient.

Dave Millar, Professional road rider and Team GB rider

	WEEK 1	WEEK 2	WEEK 3	WEEK 4
MONDAY	30–60mins Z1–Z2	30–60mins Z1–Z2	30–60mins Z1–Z2	30–60mins Z1–Z2
TUESDAY	60mins Z3, including Intervals	60mins Z3, including Pyramids	60mins Z3, including Power sprints	60mins Z3, including Reverse pyramids
WEDNESDAY	60mins Z3	60mins Z3	60mins Z3	Rest
THURSDAY	60–90mins including Leg speed intervals	60mins Power sprints	60–90mins Extended sprints	60mins Intervals
FRIDAY	Rest	Rest	Rest	Rest
SATURDAY	90–120mins Z3	120mins Z3	90mins Z3, including 4x5mins Fartlek	45mins incl. 4x60sec Z4 4x30sec Z5 6x10sec Z6
SUNDAY	180–210mins Z2–Z3	150mins Z3, incl. 2x10mins Fartlek 2x5mins Fartlek	150mins Z3, incl. 4x10mins Fartlek 4x10mins Fartlek	**RACE 80km (120mins)**
TOTAL	**8.0–10.0 hours**	**8.0–8.5 hours**	**8.0–9.0 hours**	**5.25–5.75 hours**

POINTS TO REMEMBER

· Train over terrain similar to the race venue
· Train your weak areas, develop your strengths
· Practise skills – cornering, sprinting, climbing, etc
· Use races as a learning experience – think about the areas you struggle with (hanging onto the bunch, climbing with the group, dealing with corners or sprints, etc.) and address these in subsequent training sessions.

Time Trialling

The training that you need to undertake for a time trial will vary considerably depending on the distance. To reflect this, we have included three programmes – you will see that it is about training smarter, as longer race distances do not necessarily mean longer in the saddle when training.

10-Mile

The 10-mile (16km) time trial is probably the most accessible race for anyone joining a cycle club. Many clubs run informal 'club events' over 10 or 25mi. on midweek evenings throughout the summer. At 20mph (32kph), the 10-mile trial will take 30 minutes – which is a manageable goal for almost anyone. Most time triallists spend all their training time riding at a steady pace because this is what they are striving to do when racing. However, training for short periods above race pace (e.g. intervals, fartlek, etc.) will help to develop higher speed.

Despite time trialling being a solo pursuit, it is worth trying to ride in a group at least some of the time. It will help with your speed work considerably.

The timetable opposite shows a programme to bring a rider up to speed for this short, all-out effort. Some of the preparation phase includes rides of 2–3 hours, as this foundation work is essential for all riders, and few riders specialise in such short events.

	WEEK 1	WEEK 2	WEEK 3	WEEK 4
MONDAY	30–60mins Z1–Z2	30–60mins Z1–Z2	30–60mins Z1–Z2	30–60mins Z1–Z2
TUESDAY	60mins Z3, including 400m–4km Intervals	45–60mins Z3, including Pyramids	45–60mins Z3, including Power sprints	30–60mins Z3, including Reverse pyramids
WEDNESDAY	60mins Z3	60mins Z3	60mins Z3–Z4	Rest
THURSDAY	60–90mins including Leg speed intervals	60mins Power sprints	45–60mins Extended sprints	45–60mins Intervals 200m–2km
FRIDAY	Rest	Rest	Rest	Rest
SATURDAY	90mins Z3	60mins Z3 including 4x5mins Fartlek	45–60mins Z3, including 4x150sec Z4 4x60sec Z5	30–45mins incl. 4x60sec Z4 4x30sec Z5 6x10sec Z6
SUNDAY	150–180mins Z2–Z3	120mins Z3, incl. 2x10mins Fartlek 4x5mins Fartlek	90mins Z3, incl. 4x10mins Fartlek 4x10mins Fartlek	**RACE 10m TT (20–30mins)**
TOTAL	**7.5–9.0 hours**	**6.25–7.0 hours**	**5.25–6.5 hours**	**2.75–4.25 hours**

POINTS TO REMEMBER

· In the last couple of weeks, train on your race bike, set up for time trialling (unless riding with a group, when aerobars should not be used)
· Use a variety of terrains – downhill slopes or wind-assisted roads to develop speed and uphill slopes or headwinds to help develop power
· Use a heart rate monitor to help maintain a steady effort – remember that in a race you will probably be able to maintain a heart rate about 10bpm above your training heart rate.

25-Mile

Although two and a half times further than a 10-mile time trial, the preparation for a '25' (40km) is not vastly different.

If you are already used to riding for more hours in a week, it is feasible to do more hours of training, but the principles of tapering should still apply.

	WEEK 1	WEEK 2	WEEK 3	WEEK 4
MONDAY	60–90mins Z1–Z2	60–90mins Z1–Z2	60–90mins Z1–Z2	45–60mins Z1–Z2
TUESDAY	60mins Z3, including 400m–4km Intervals	45–60mins Z3, including Pyramids	45–60mins Z3, including Power sprints	30–60mins Z3, including Reverse pyramids
WEDNESDAY	90mins Z3	90mins Z3	60–90mins Z3–Z4	Rest
THURSDAY	60–90mins including Leg speed intervals	60mins Power sprints	45–60mins Extended sprints	45–60mins Intervals 200m–2km
FRIDAY	Rest	Rest	Rest	Rest
SATURDAY	90mins Z3	60mins Z3 including 4x5mins Fartlek	45–60 mins Z3, incl. 4x150sec Z4 4x60sec Z5 6x10sec Z6	30–45mins incl. 4x60sec Z4 4x30sec Z5 6x10sec Z6
SUNDAY	150–180mins Z2–Z3	150mins Z3, incl. 2x10mins Fartlek 4x5mins Fartlek	90mins Z3, incl. 4x10mins Fartlek 4x10mins Fartlek	**RACE 25m TT (~60mins)**
TOTAL	**7.0–10.5 hours**	**7.75–8.5 hours**	**5.75–7.5 hours**	**3.5–4.75 hours**

50–100-Mile

Longer time trials demand greater stamina and more time spent 'getting the miles in', especially during the winter and early spring. Most '50s' (80km) and '100s' (160km) are held once the warmer weather has arrived. As a consequence, they tend to be held once the racing season is well underway, and so need to be slotted in among other events.

	WEEK 1	WEEK 2	WEEK 3	WEEK 4
MONDAY	45–60mins Z1–Z2	30–60mins Z1–Z2	45–60mins Z1–Z2	45–60mins Z1–Z2
TUESDAY	45–60mins Z3, Leg speed Intervals	45–90mins Chaingang or Fartlek session	30–60mins Z3, including Power sprints	45–90mins Chaingang or Fartlek session
WEDNESDAY	10m TT (20–30mins)	10m TT (20–30mins)	10m TT (20–30mins)	10m TT (20–30mins)
THURSDAY	45–60mins including Extended sprints	45–60mins Intervals 200m–2km	45–90mins Chaingang or Fartlek session	30–45mins including Reverse pyramids
FRIDAY	Rest	Rest	Rest	Rest
SATURDAY	30–45mins incl. 4x60sec Z4 4x30sec Z5 6x10sec Z6	45mins incl. 4x60sec Z4 4x30sec Z5 6x10sec Z6	30–45mins incl. 4x60sec Z 4x30sec Z5 6x10sec Z6	Rest or 30–60mins Z1–Z2
SUNDAY	RACE 25m TT (~60mins)	RACE 50m (~2.0hrs)	RACE 25m TT (~60mins)	RACE 100m TT (~4.0–5.0hrs)
TOTAL	4.0–5.25 hours	5.0–6.75 hours	3.25–5.75 hours	7.0–9.75 hours

POINTS TO REMEMBER

· Train using the food and drink you expect to use during the race
· Have a pacing strategy – it is better to start steadily and increase pace to absolute maximum in the last 10 miles (16km), than to start too quickly and expire with 10 miles still to race
· For the 100m TT, it may be worth raising the handlebars by 1-2cm for a more comfortable position
· See how the total hours of training and racing a generally reduced in this part of season – because the intensity is greatly increased.

Track

As we saw in *Chapter 4*, there is a huge range of track events. However, they basically fall into two categories – sprint and endurance. We have included a training programme for each.

Sprint

Just because track sprint events are of a short duration, that doesn't mean they are an easy option in terms of training. Top sprinters spend hours each week working on their strength, speed and tactics. If you don't have regular access to a velodrome, you'll need to supplement your training with other events and specific training drills.

The plan shown here is designed around preparation for a rider who wishes to specialise in sprint events in a Tuesday evening local track league but also rides road races and time trials.

The events that this programme would cover include 200m time trial, 500m time trial, 1km time trial, team sprint, match sprint and keirin.

My tips for sprinting:
1. Pedal fast
2. Pedal smooth
3. Get strong
4. Eat well
5. Easy on the beers

Craig McLean, World and
European team sprint champion

	WEEK 1	WEEK 2	WEEK 3	WEEK 4	WEEK 5	WEEK 6
MON	Easy ride 30–60mins	Easy ride 30–60mins	Easy ride 30–60mins	Easy ride 30–60mins	Easy ride 30–60mins	Easy ride 30–60mins
TUE	60–90mins, including Leg speed intervals	60–90mins Extended sprints	60mins Power sprints	**Track league**	**Track league**	**Track league**
WED	Easy ride 30–60mins	Easy ride 30–60mins	Easy ride 30–60mins	Easy ride 30–60mins	Easy ride 30–60mins	Easy ride 30–60mins
THU	10mins TT or 90mins Z3, including Power sprints	10mins TT or 90mins Z3, Extended 4x5mins Fartlek	10mins TT or 45–60mins Intervals sprints	10mins TT or 45–60mins Chaingang or 60m–300m	10mins TT or 45–90mins Z3, including Fartlek session	10mins TT or Road 60mins Pyramids
FRI	Rest	Rest	Rest	Rest	Rest	Rest
SAT	Road 90–120mins Z3	Road 45mins inc. 5x12sec Z6 6x10sec Z6 8x8sec Z6 10x6sec Z6	Road 12mins Z3	45–60mins Intervals 60m–300m	Road 45mins, inc. 5x12sec Z6 6x10sec Z6 8x8sec Z6 10x6sec Z6	30–45mins, including Reverse pyramids
SUN	10–25m TT or 60–120mins road race	10–25m TT or 60–120mins road race	10–25m TT or 60–120mins road race	10–25m TT or 60–120mins road race	10–25m TT or 60–120mins road race	10–25m TT or 60–120mins road race
TOTAL	5.5–9.0 hours	5.25–7.75 hours	5.75–8.0 hours	3.5–6.0 hours plus league	3.5–6.25 hours plus league	3.5–5.75 hours plus league

The track bike is the purest form of cycling – no gears, no brakes.

Chris Hoy, World and Olympic 1km champion

Endurance

Like the track sprinter's programme above, the plan below is worked around a Tuesday evening track league. However, the endurance rider is encouraged to tackle more endurance events and drills such as road races up to about 3 hours, time trials up to 25mi. (40km), chaingang training sessions, and a mixture of long- and short-distance high intensity speed work.

The events that this programme would cover include pursuit, team pursuit, points race, scratch race, devil and Madison.

	WEEK 1	WEEK 2	WEEK 3	WEEK 4	WEEK 5	WEEK 6
MON	Easy ride 30–60mins	Easy ride 30–60mins	Easy ride 30–60mins	Easy ride 30–60mins	Easy ride 30–60mins	Easy ride 30–60mins
TUE	60–90mins, including Leg speed intervals	60–90mins Power sprints	60mins Chaingang or Fartlek session	**Track league**	**Track league**	**Track league**
WED	Easy ride 30–60mins	Easy ride 30–60mins	Easy ride 30–60mins	Easy ride 30–60mins	Easy ride 30–60mins	Easy ride 30–60mins
THU	10mins TT or 90mins Z3, including Power sprints	10mins TT or 90mins Z3, Extended 4x5mins Fartlek	10mins TT or 45–60mins Intervals sprints	10mins TT or 45–60mins Chaingang or 60m–300m	10mins TT or 45–90mins Z3, including Fartlek session	10mins TT or Road 60mins Pyramids
FRI	Rest	Rest	Rest	Rest	Rest	Rest
SAT	Road 90–120mins Z3, including 4x5mins Fartlek	Road 45mins, including 4x60sec Z5 8x30sec Z5 12x10sec Z6	Road 2.0hrs Z3, including 2x5mins and 2x10mins Fartlek	45–60mins Intervals 60m–300m	Road 45mins, inc. 2x60sec Z5 4x30sec Z6 8x20sec Z6 10x10sec Z6	Road 30–45mins, including Reverse pyramids
SUN	120–180mins road race	120–180mins road race	60–150mins road race	60–150mins road race	60–150mins road race	60–150mins road race
TOTAL	7–10.0 hours	6.25–8.25 hours	5.5–9.0 hours	3.5–6.5 hours plus league	3.5–6.75 hours plus league	3.5–6.25 hours plus league

Mountain bike racing

Mountain bike racing broadly falls into two categories: cross country and downhill. Here we look at just cross country events, as downhill racing is more concerned with quick-handling skills (which are best dealt with by a hands-on, practical approach from a coach) rather than the endurance conditioning requirements of the cross-country rider which can more easily be given as general instructions.

90-minute Race

Just like racing on the road, the effort of a 90-minute off-road race is vastly different to that of an hour and half's leisure ride. 90 minutes is a typical duration for a sport rider racing off-road – although this may vary by 15–20 minutes either way depending on the course conditions and the fitness of the rider. Before embarking on a long competitive ride it's worth building up your endurance abilities with a bank of steady-paced off-road rides under your wheels. In addition, this will help improve your technical skills. The table below shows a good programme for the transition period from late-February to a first event at the beginning of April.

	WEEK 1	WEEK 2	WEEK 3	WEEK 4	WEEK 5	WEEK 6
MON	Road or turbo 30–60mins Z1-2	Road or turbo 30–60mins Z1-2	Road or turbo 30–60mins Z1-2	Road or turbo 30–60mins Z1-2	Road 30–60mins Z1-Z2 skills	Road 30–60mins Z1-Z2 skills
TUE	Gym or weights	Gym or weights	Gym or weights	Gym or weights	Gym or weights	Gym or weights
WED	60minsZ3	60minsZ3	60minsZ3	Skills	Skills	Rest
THU	Road 60–90mins including Leg speed intervals	Road 60mins, Power sprints	Road 60–90mins Extended sprints	Road 60mins Z3, including Intervals	Rest	Road 30–45mins Intervals
FRI	Rest	Rest	Rest	Rest	Rest	Rest
SAT	Road 90–120mins Z3,	Road 120mins Z3	Road 90mins Z3, including 4x5mins Fartlek	Off-road 90mins Z3, including Power sprints	Off-road 60mins Z3, including Pyramids	Road 45mins, including 4x60sec Z4 4x30sec Z5 6x10sec Z6
SUN	Off-road 210–240mins Z2-Z3	Off-road 240mins Z2-Z3	Off-road 150–180mins Z3, including 2x10mins and 2x5mins Fartlek	Off-road 120–150mins Z3, including 4x10mins Fartlek	Off-road 90–120mins Z3, including 4x10mins Fartlek	**RACE 90-mins**
TOTAL	8–10.0 hours	8.0–8.5 hours	8.0–9.0 hours	5.25–5.75 hours	3.0–4.0 hours	3.25–4.0 hours

Six-hour Enduro

Mountain bike enduro events are usually a long loop and can cover almost any length. Like their road counterparts – the sportive rides – the head of the field is a hard-fought affair with riders battling it out with all the cut and thrust of any competition. For the rest of the field, it is merely a test of their endurance (or survival) abilities.

A foundation of progressively longer rides is essential. Assuming this background of rides up to, say, 3 hours, the programme below would help anyone tackle an enduro expected to last about 6 hours (approximately 80–100km, 50–65mi.) without intending to be 'up there' with the front-runners.

	WEEK 1	WEEK 2	WEEK 3	WEEK 4	WEEK 5	WEEK 6
MON	Road or turbo 30–60mins Z1-2	Road or turbo 30–60mins Z1-2	Road or turbo 30–60mins Z1-2	Road or turbo 30–60mins Z1-2	Road or turbo 30–60mins Z1-2	Road or turbo 30–60mins Z1-2
TUE	Road or off-road 45–75mins Z1-2	Road or off-road 45–75mins Z1-2	Road or off-road 60–90mins Z1-2	Road or off-road 60–90mins Z1-2	Road 1–2hrs Z1-Z2	Road 30–60mins Z1-Z2
WED	Rest or easy ride	Rest or easy ride	Rest or easy ride	Rest or easy ride	Rest or easy ride	Rest or easy ride
THU	Road 30–60mins Z1-2	Road 45–60mins Z1-2	Road 45–75mins Z1-2	Road 45–60mins Z1-2	Road 1–2hrs Z1-2	Road 30–60mins Z1-2
FRI	Rest	Rest	Rest	Rest	Rest	Rest
SAT	Rest or easy ride	60–90mins easy ride	90–120mins easy ride	90–120mins easy ride	120–150mins easy ride	60–90mins easy ride
SUN	180–210mins off-road	180–240mins off-road	3.5–5.0hrs road	210–270mins off-road	180–240mins road	**RACE**
TOTAL	8–10.0 hours	8.0–8.5 hours	8.0–9.0 hours	5.25–5.75 hours	3.0–4.0 hours	3.25–4.0 hours

24-hour Relay

Team enduro races are popular and fun. There's something magical about riding through the day, into the dusk and darkness and following morning's sunrise. Even though you will have familiarised yourself with the course by riding a number of laps in daylight, the same paths can appear quite alien when tackled in the dark and illuminated only by your lights.

The more members in your team, the fewer laps you will have to cover individually. But if you're doing fewer laps, your team-mates will expect you to ride them faster. Every lap has to be ridden close to a regular race pace. The upside of this is that you get longer to rest. Pity the poor souls who have elected to ride the event as solo riders.

One lap of a typical relay event will usually take 45–60 minutes to cover. If the team has more than two members, it is normal to swap riders every lap. If there are only two riders in the team, you might elect to swap riders every two laps, so that you do not lose any time with more frequent transitions and so that you both can have longer rest breaks.

The composition of your team will therefore dictate your training strategy. With three or four members, you'll need to ride fast, but you'll have 2–3 hours' rest between each lap. Two-person teams will need to spend more time developing their endurance capabilities.

The following are training strategies rather than programmes – they give you a rough guide of the sort of training that you will need to consider in the months leading up to the race and the training hours you need to put in. They are based on the event taking place in July.

POINTS TO REMEMBER

- Ride with others – if they are better at some technical skills than you, ask them to help you master these aspects
- Practise your technical skills at race pace or faster
- Train your weak areas, develop your strengths
- Pace yourself – it is far better to have a slow start and then to catch and pass others in the later stages of the race than to lead in the beginning and be passed by most of the field later on
- Allow yourself time to recover from off-road rides
- Use gym training or weights to develop upper-body strength.

Two-person team training strategy

Training cycle	Preparation		Transition	Overload	Tapering & peak	
Month	February	March	April	May	June	July
2–3 hour off-road rides	✔	✔	2 ✔			RACE
Skills training	✔	✔	✔	✔	✔	✔
MTB races		✔	✔	✔	✔	✔
Enduro rides			✔	✔	✔	✔
Short road races or TTs				✔	✔	✔
Weekly training hours	5–10	7–12	9–14	10–16	10–14	8–14

Three- or four-person training strategy
This is similar to that of the two-person team but with more emphasis on speed work. Hence the introduction of short road races or time trials in April and less emphasis on enduro rides.

Training cycle	Preparation		Transition	Overload	Tapering & peak	
Month	February	March	April	May	June	July
2–3 hour off-road rides	✔	✔	✔			RACE
Skills training	✔	✔	✔	✔	✔	✔
MTB races		✔	✔	✔	✔	✔
Enduro rides			✔	✔	✔	✔
Short road races or TTs			✔	✔	✔	✔
Weekly training hours	5–10	6–12	8–14	10–14	10–14	8–14

POINTS TO REMEMBER

· Use the early season as an opportunity to develop your endurance and do shorter, more intense rides closer to the event
· Taper the volume of training and increase the intensity of training in the 2–3 weeks before the competition
· Use your training rides to experiment with different race foods
· Divide your training between on-road and off-road – you need off-road skills, but road riding will help to develop your speed more easily and it doesn't batter your body quite as much, so you can train more
· Be flexible – if one of your team-mates becomes tired or injured, you may need to do extra laps.

Cyclo-cross

Cyclo-cross events are short – approximately one hour – and quick. Apart from riding a bike over rough terrain, they involve short sections of running with the bike, hurdling obstacles, and a high degree of bike handling skills. All of these elements need to be incorporated in the training programme. The sample programme here takes a rider up to their first event of the season, using the closing events of the road or mountain bike racing season as preparation.

	WEEK 1	WEEK 2	WEEK 3	WEEK 4
MONDAY	30–60mins Z1–Z2	30–60mins Recovery Z1	45–60mins Z1–Z2 20–30mins Running	45–60mins Weight training 20–30mins Running
TUESDAY	60mins, including Reverse pyramids	30–45mins, including Pyramids	45–90mins Chaingang or Fartlek session	60min Skills training
WEDNESDAY	20–30mins Running	60mins Skills training	60mins Skills training	60min SIntervals
THURSDAY	45–60mins Chaingang or Fartlek session	Rest	Rest	30mins Running, inc. 4x120m, 4x60m 6x30m sprints
FRIDAY	Rest	30mins Running, including 4x120m, 4x60m sprints	30mins Running, including 4x120m, 4x60m 6x30m sprints	Rest
SATURDAY	45mins Running, 4x60sec Z4 4x30sec Z5 6x10sec Z6	60–120mins Skills training	60–120mins Skills training	45mins incl. 4x60sec Z4 4x30sec Z5 6x10sec Z6
SUNDAY	Race 120mins (Road or MTB)	60–90mins Off-road ride Z2-Z3, including Skills training close to race pace	60–90mins Off-road ride Z2-Z3, including Skills training at/over race pace	**RACE (60mins)**
TOTAL	**5.5–5.75 hours**	**4.0–6.75 hours**	**5.25–8.0 hours**	**5.0–5.75 hours**

POINTS TO REMEMBER

· A fast start is essential – hence the intervals and running sprints
· Skills training must be given due time and attention – some of this needs to be done at high intensity but equally can be included on more moderate intensity rides
· Weight training will help deal with handling the bike on rough terrain as well as shouldering it for steep climbs or obstacles
· If racing in the summer as well, you need to allow yourself some recovery time either during the season, or at the end of it, before the cyclo-cross racing begins; plus another recovery period after the cyclo-cross season before the next summer season of racing.

Cyclo-sportive

The breadth of events that can fall under this discipline really is vast, so you do need to develop specific training programmes for the event in question. To give you a rough idea of the planning that is needed, here are a couple of examples.

The Etape du Tour

This event has really captured the imagination of both amateur racing cyclists and tourists seeking a challenge. It is an opportunity for cyclists to experience a stage of the Tour de France. It is held over one of the mountain stages with three or four major climbs in a distance of 180–250km (110–160mi.).

Even though many riders are likely to be travelling at half the speed of the pros who will tackle exactly the same route on the following day, the Étape is not to be taken lightly.

Although most of the climbs of the Alps, Pyrenees or Massif Central are not particularly steep, they can easily take two hours or more to ascend. This needs some good quality preparation if a rider is going to have a successful day emulating his or her cycling heroes.

A lightweight bike is a must. Even experienced racing cyclists will appreciate the benefits of some seriously low gears (in their terms) – 39 x 27 or 39 x 29 are both a good option. More mortal riders will probably benefit from a compact double chainset with an inner ring of 36 or 34 teeth, or even a triple chainset with an inner chainring of 32 or 30 teeth. You may not need such low gears – and indeed, will travel faster if using bigger gears whenever possible – but after a long, arduous day in the saddle, climbing up the final pass into a headwind you'll be grateful for those extra few teeth on the bottom sprocket or that almost toothless 'granny ring'.

If you are considering riding the Etape (which takes place in July), then you need to start serious preparation by the previous December. The first few months can concentrate on building up the hours on the bike. By April you should increase the intensity of your rides, not only tackling distances faster but heading into hillier countryside. You may not have an Alp to train on nearby, but it's worth seeking whatever hills you can get to. Consider entering local Audax or cyclo-sportive events that take you over more challenging terrain, or arrange a weekend in the hills.

The table below gives an indication of a good build-up of longest rides (in km) you should be scheduling in preparation for this event. In addition to these distances, you need to be riding a similar total distance in 2–5 shorter sessions each week – thus doubling the total weekly distance.

In the winter, this may be difficult to do safely or in reasonable weather, in which case some of these rides can be substituted with turbo training, spinning classes, weight training or gym activities. By March, however, all training should be on the bike.

TRAINING CYCLE		Preparation				Recovery	Overload		Tapering & peak	
MONTH		Nov	Dec	Jan	Feb	Mar	Apr	May	Jun	Jul
WEEK	1	60	75	100	110	120	160	200	200	180
	2	60	90	110	120	100	120	140	160	120
	3	80	100	90	100	140	180	160	210	**RACE**
	4			120	130		160	180	230	

POINTS TO REMEMBER

· Make sure you get your entry sent off as early as possible – this event gets filled up very quickly
· Use these rides to develop your eating and drinking strategies
· Where possible, train with others – riding in company will help your motivation, particularly when the weather is not looking too kind (plus, you're unlikely to be riding the event alone so it's worth getting used to riding amongst some other wheels)
· Don't despair if your times don't compare well with those of the pros – few do!

Long-distance Leisure Ride

If you are new to cycling and desire to ride further than your immediate horizon, 80–160km (50–100mi.) in a day is a manageable goal. There are many organised events that make for a perfect introduction to cycling longer distances – in the UK, the annual London–Brighton charity ride is 88km (55mi.) long, with a sting in the tail – climbing over the South Downs at Ditchling Beacon. A fit racing cyclist could cover

this distance in around 2 hours, but that's not the point. The event allows you to take all day to cover the distance and enjoy the experience.

You don't need to give yourself the 9-month preparation time of the racing cyclists aiming to peak at a major event, but 9 weeks from a zero-cycling base is a good idea, largely to help you get used to sitting on a saddle for the 4–8 hours that this journey may take.

If you are going to invest in some cycling gear, shorts and a helmet are the wisest purchases. Have your bike checked over by a specialist bike shop where staff can check your riding position and advise you on appropriate equipment, such as fitting 'slick' tyres to a mountain bike instead of off-road 'knobblies', suitable tyre pressures and using the gears on your bike.
The most important advice: start training. Don't worry about distance at first, 20–60

minutes pedalling may be more than enough initially. You need to pace yourself – if you feel yourself struggling for breath, slow down. Use a lower gear so that you're pedalling a little faster, but more easily. Racing cyclists' cadence is around 90-100rpm yours should be similar but using lower gears (expect this to drop when climbing).

Ideally, you need to get on your bike 2–4 times each week. Every second ride, increase the time by 10–20 minutes. After the third week, you should be able to ride 60–120 minutes without too much difficulty – progress does come quickly if you hang in there. You may find it easier to schedule midweek rides as reasonably short distances (or consider cycling to work), but increase the distance on one weekend day. Vary the duration of your rides and try to ride a little faster over the shorter distances. You'll soon be getting fitter and quicker and have greater endurance.
The following schedule aims to get you in shape for an event such as the London-Brighton ride. Notice how it 'tapers' in Week 8, before the Target ride, so that you are not too exhausted for your goal. Also, Week 5 is an easy week to allow your body time to recover after building a solid foundation over the first four weeks.

TRAINING CYCLE	Preparation				Recovery	Overload		Tapering & peak	
WEEK	1	2	3	4	5	6	7	8	9
	30	30	45	45	60	45	45	60	45
RIDE DURATION (MINS)	30	45	60	60	90	60	60	60	60
	45	45	60	90	90	90	120	120	
			90	120		150	180	60	TARGET

POINTS TO REMEMBER

- Take a drink with you, especially on any ride of 40 minutes or more
- You may also need to eat some food on rides of over 60 minutes
- Vary your routes, both for interest and to train over different terrains
- Avoid busy roads – quiet roads are safer and tend to be more interesting for cycling (use the opportunity to explore your local area!)
- On longer rides (of over 90 minutes) you may want to rest for a while – don't stop for too long (5–15 minutes) or your muscles will cool and you'll have difficulty starting off again
- Pace yourself – aim to ride at a consistent pace throughout your rides, rather than always covering the second half in a slower time.

600km Randonnée

This is the longest standard distance in the audax calendar. The time limits are 20–40 hours. Of course, it pays to have built up to this length of ride by completing plenty of 200km (125mi.), 300km (190mi.) and one or two 400km (250mi.) events before you embark on a journey of this length.

Many randonneurs wisely spend a season riding no more than 200km events before they tackle an overnight ride. Events beyond 300km are usually held between the end of April and the end of August for reasons of daylight, better weather and to allow riders to get physically prepared for these marathon rides.

Good preparatory distances are vital. If you begin your campaign with 200km rides in February or March, that will prepare you for the more demanding events later. It is not necessary to push yourself to ride the longest event available every weekend. In fact your performances will soon decline if you do attempt that. Do give yourself time to recover from the longer rides.

The table below gives an indication of a good build-up of longest rides (in km) you should be scheduling in preparation for this event.

Training is important, but it is pointless if you don't take enough rest.

Dean Downing, Professional road rider

TRAINING CYCLE		Progressive preparation (including recovery periods)				Recovery		Overload		Tapering & peak
MONTH		1	2	3	4	5	6	7	8	9
	1	60		70	120	120	200	400	200	300
	2	60	70	80	100	200	200	100	400	200
WEEK	**3**	80	80	90	100	200		200	200	
	4	80	90	100	90	120	300	300		**TARGET**

Keeping Healthy

Introduction

Health and fitness are two separate things – and this is a point often overlooked by many cyclists. You may have identified your physical strengths, honed your skills, and spent long hours on your bike and in the gym, but this hard-earned cycling fitness will mean nothing unless you are healthy.

This chapter will look at the health issues related to cycling. Broadly speaking, these fall into two categories:

- nutrition and hydration – quite simply, your engine (i.e. your body) won't run unless you keep it fuelled
- aches and pains – this is a catalogue of typical injuries, health concerns and niggles that we must endure in the name of our sport.

Nutrition and hydration

Food is the cyclist's fuel. Many riders spend a fortune on their bicycle equipment but ignore their 'fuel'. The truth is that most riders would perform much better if they paid more attention to the correct fuelling of their 'engines' rather than worrying about the merits of the latest frameset, tyre or seatpost.

Balanced diet

There is a great deal of information in our day-to-day lives about what we should eat and, just as importantly, what we shouldn't – five portions of fruit and vegetables a day, cut out the doughnuts and cut down on the alcohol. And then there are the classic cycling diet tips – eat as much pasta as you can lay your hands on. But if you follow a few basic rules, you will find it easy to keep a balanced diet.

Essentially, all you need to do is follow the 'Balance of Good Health' model based on UK Government recommendations from 1992. This model states that you should strive for the following balance in your diet:

- 5 or more portions of fruit and vegetables – accounting for about 33% of your diet each day
- 5–11 portions of bread, other cereals and potatoes – 34%
- 2–3 portions of dairy foods – 15%
- 2–3 portions of protein-rich foods such as chicken, fish, eggs and lentils – 12%
- 1–3 portions of essential oils such as oily fish and some nuts and seeds – 7%.

Of course, the size of a portion of fruit compared to a portion of essential oil will differ, but if you keep to the suggested balance you will find that you get all the micronutrients, vitamins, minerals and fibre that you need.

Fuels for cycling

As a cyclist, it is likely that your chief concern when it comes to food – after how good it tastes – is how much energy it can supply. Essentially, there are four components in food and drink that are capable of producing energy:
- carbohydrate
- protein
- fat
- alcohol.

A single gramme of each component produces a different amount of energy, commonly expressed in kilocalories (kcal) or simply as calories (Cal) (although to be technically correct, energy should be expressed in kilojoules (1kcal = 4.2kj)). So, one gramme of each component will produce:
- carbohydrate = 4kcal
- protein = 4kcal
- fat = 9kcal
- alcohol = 7kcal.

The calories supplied by each component can be used by the body with differing degrees of success – so you can't take your fill on fat and alcohol thinking that this is the most effective way of taking on your energy supplies. Carbohydrate is the body's preferred source of fuel, followed by protein (after carbohydrate stores have been exhausted). Alcohol cannot be used directly by the muscles but is broken down at a fixed rate by the liver. The majority of fat is stored around the organs of the body and under the skin.

In terms of the balance of these components in your diet, this will depend on the specifics of your own training and riding discipline – for example endurance riding will demand more carbohydrate, while a programme aimed at building muscle strength and bulk will require and increase in protein. However, you should roughly aim at:
- carbohydrate = 60%
- protein = 18%
- (healthy) fat = 22%

At the risk of sounding like a government education programme – if in doubt about what you are eating, always read the label.

The number of calories you need to take on board each day will depend on your size, metabolic rate, ambient temperature and a range of other factors. But most of all it will depend on your activity levels. In normal daily activity an adult male needs about 2,500kcal per day. A more active person may use 3,000kcal or more. A rider in the Tour de France or Race Across America will use 6,000–8,000kcal per day! And these need to be replaced if he is to ride the following day. Taking on board this volume of calories – particularly in a healthy, balanced diet – can become pretty difficult. An adult female typically needs fewer calories a day – in the region of 1,900kcal.

Carbohydrate

This is your body's preferred source of energy and long-distance riders will need as much as 70% of their total energy intake from carbohydrates. Carbohydrate is stored as glycogen in the muscles and liver. Roughly 1,600–2,000kcal can be stored in the body – enough to last about one day if you ate nothing. The glycogen is readily accessible for energy use but unless topped up during exercise, these carbohydrate stores will only last about two hours.

Cycling is predominantly an aerobic activity. Road races and off-road events may involve occasional sprints or difficult climbs, close to an anaerobic effort, but for the vast majority of the time the pace is sustainable – where the energy demand is similar to the supply of oxygen to the muscles and the body can burn a mixture of carbohydrate and fat.

At low levels of exercise intensity, more fats are metabolised than carbohydrates. As the pace increases, so the amount of fat used diminishes and carbohydrate becomes the main fuel source. In anaerobic activity (e.g. very high intensity sprinting) carbohydrates are the principal energy source and no energy comes from fat.

As the duration of exercise continues, your body will use more fat stores and less carbohydrate. Your body will initially use carbohydrate stores but as these become depleted it will try to conserve the muscle glycogen (some carbohydrate is required in order to metabolise the fat into energy) and will switch to the glycogen in the liver. Muscle proteins will then begin to break down to help meet energy demands. Such chemical reactions in the body are expensive in terms of energy demands and so it is preferable firstly to begin exercising with properly topped-up glycogen stores by having eaten a meal high in carbohydrates before exercise and, secondly, to keep your muscle glycogen stores continually topped up by eating and drinking appropriate carbohydrate-rich food and drinks.

The fitter you are, the better your muscles become at using fat and sparing the glycogen within the muscles. Less trained riders will use their glycogen faster and so will tire more quickly – it's known as 'getting the bonk' in cycling circles or 'hitting the wall' in marathon running, when you feel that your energy reserves are utterly exhausted. In fact, you have enough calories secreted about your body for about 10 days' survival, but the readily processed calories for exercise just aren't available. Everyone can benefit from high glycogen levels, to ride harder and for longer.

GOOD SOURCES OF CARBOHYDRATES INCLUDE:

- Cereals
- Bread, pasta, rice, potatoes
- Beans, peas, lentils
- Fruit – fresh, dried, tinned, juice and smoothies
- Jam, honey
- Sports products – in drink, bar and gel form

Protein

Protein is needed for the creation of new bone, muscle and skin. Active people – and cyclists definitely come into this category – do need higher levels of protein intake than sedentary people to regenerate tissue (muscle) and red blood cells, and keep their bones healthy.

Protein can be used as an energy source for the muscles but the energy produced from burning protein is relatively small. In extreme cases, the body will break down its own muscle protein to be used as a source of energy if there are insufficient carbohydrate and fat sources available (this may occur in intensive riding such as the stage races or extended touring).

Your diet should be approximately 15–20% protein, depending on your personal requirements. Eating larger quantities of protein is not beneficial but is excreted as urea, placing a greater strain on the kidneys. If you have a high-protein diet it is important to increase your fluid intake. Like any food, if you eat more protein than your body can cope with, it will simply store the excess as fat.

Fat

Fat is an essential part of anyone's diet. Fat metabolises the fat-soluble vitamins A, D, E and K and having nine calories per gramme compared to the four of carbohydrates and proteins, it is a rich source of energy. However, fat slows down your digestion so is not good in foods for a quick energy boost. Plus, your body will convert any excess food to fat if there is an energy surplus. Your body needs 'essential fatty acids' which can only be supplied by the diet in the form of unsaturated fats.

A healthy sports diet can be composed of 15–30%. Limit your intake of saturated fats (typically, fat that is solid at room temperature) though, as these have been linked to increased cholesterol and heart disease problems. Stay well clear of trans-fats and hydrogenated fats too.

Alcohol

Too much alcohol is bad news for serious bike riders. The calories from alcohol are stored almost immediately as fat – and that does not 'burn off' as quickly as energy stored as muscle glycogen. As a consequence, riders who enjoy a few too many drinks may find themselves struggling with their weight. Not only that, but alcohol impairs your reaction times, balance and coordination, body temperature regulation, power and endurance. It's a diuretic and taken after exercise it can reduce your body's ability to rehydrate.

Don't despair, though an occasional beer or glass of wine won't harm you (and some studies show there are even benefits to drinking moderate amounts of alcohol) and it may help to relax you the night before an event or to wind down once you are suitably fed and watered after a race.

Micronutrients

Vitamins, minerals and trace elements are 'micronutrients' vital for the body's functions including cell metabolism and generation – they help wounds to heal and bolster the immune system as well as contributing to stave off infection, conduct nerve impulses, blood coagulation and control the body's fluid balance and a host other minor, but absolutely essential, roles in the body.

Vitamins A, D, E and K are soluble in fat, and vitamins B and C are soluble in water. All are prevalent in fruit and vegetables. In very simple terms, eating the government-recommended five portions of fruit and vegetables (excluding potatoes from the vegetable list) per day is sufficient to provide a healthy balance. Choose foods of different colours and textures to give wider nutritional intake.

Think of the Periodic Table studied in your school science lessons and you have a good idea of what minerals are: calcium, copper, chromium, iron, magnesium, manganese, potassium, sodium, zinc, etc. The key essential minerals for cyclists are calcium, iron and zinc. Calcium is required for bone regeneration and can be obtained from dairy products. Iron helps transport oxygen throughout the body and hence is vital to avoid feeling fatigued. Zinc helps the breakdown and use of carbohydrate

Too much alcohol is definitely a bad thing, but a beer or two after a big day in the saddle is just reward.

Be sure to take on water before, during and after your riding.

and in protein synthesis. It also maintains a strong immune system and helps to build muscle, thus is important for endurance athletes.

It is, however, very difficult to get the balance of minerals right. Deficiencies are best identified through blood tests. The other problem is that not all vitamins and minerals work well together. For example, aluminium (found in many deodorants) depletes the body of magnesium (key to muscle and nerve functioning, tissue repair and muscle growth); chromium aids insulin to regulate fat and glucose metabolism but its absorption is decreased by iron, magnesium and zinc; copper strengthens connective tissue, ligaments and tendons but its absorption is decreased by calcium, iron, molybdenum, vitamin C and zinc. The list goes on.

Hydration

A sedentary person needs about 2–2.5l of water per day (directly as liquid and indirectly through foodstuffs), but if you are active in hot conditions your fluid requirement can increase to as much as eight times this figure. As you exercise you produce heat and sweat evaporates from the skin to regulate your body temperature. Unless replaced by drinking, sweat loss will lead to dehydration, impaired performances, poor recovery and a greater likelihood of picking up infections.

The usual rule of thumb is to drink 500ml of liquid per hour, but double this for hot weather or humid conditions when you sweat more. You need to drink in cool weather too – exercise still produces heat. In very cold conditions you can see your breath condensing as you breathe out, showing that you lose moisture just by breathing. Keep drinking small amounts – 'little and often' – to maintain your fluid balance.

It is vital to be properly hydrated before you exercise and to continue drinking throughout the event as much as possible. Thirst is not a good indicator of needing to drink. If you feel thirsty, then you are already beginning to dehydrate. Studies have shown that even low levels of dehydration will lead to a loss of around 10% of your capacity to ride and will cause premature fatigue (Colgan, 1990) due to:

- reduction in blood volume
- decreased skin blood flow
- decreased sweat rate
- decreased heat dissipation
- increased body core temperature
- increased rate of muscle glycogen usage.

A soigneur waits for his team to pass 'lunch' to the riders who need several thousand calories a day.

Other consequences of dehydration include:

- muscle cramps
- gastric distress
- increased blood viscosity, putting more strain on the heart
- reduced immune system defences
- risk of heat stroke, organ failure and – when body fluid losses approach 12–15% – death (Muehling, 1994).

What to drink

For rides of less than 60 minutes, water or diluted squash is quite adequate to replace fluid losses. For longer, or particularly hot, rides with greater sweat losses, sports drinks containing carbohydrate are a better option. Ordinary fruit juices and squash drinks can cause dehydration unless diluted, as they are usually too concentrated for ready absorption and require the body's existing water content to dilute them before they can be used.

After exercise and on longer rides, there is a case for replenishing the body's micronutrients with drinks containing electrolytes (sodium and potassium salts that you lose through sweating). Don't panic if you cannot always obtain your favourite electrolyte replacement drink – sweat is more dilute than plasma so electrolyte replacement is not as essential as simple fluid replacement. In other words, plain water is better than nothing.

In temperate conditions you can usually manage with two bottles carrying 500–750ml each, enough for a 2–3 hours. On longer rides you will need to be resupplied along the route either by helpers, at feed-stations or by stopping at a shop, café or bar to buy drinks and fill up your bottles.

In hot conditions or in greater humidity, and in more remote regions, you will have to carry more liquid with you either by taking extra bottles on your bike (or, at a push, in your pockets) or use a hydration pack like the Camelbak or Platypus.

Types of fluid

Fluid is absorbed into the body through the stomach. Drinks are described as isotonic, hypotonic or hypertonic depending on how rapidly they move from the stomach into the bloodstream.

- Isotonic drinks are 'in balance' with the body's fluid levels and empty easily from the gut into the bloodstream. Typically, isotonic sports drinks contain 5–8% carbohydrate (5–8g carbohydrate per 100ml). Sodium helps absorption and these drinks can be consumed at any time without hindering hydration.
- Hypotonic drinks empty from the gut even faster, but they tend to have low levels of minerals or carbohydrate. They are very useful for hydration – especially in hot conditions. These drinks are usually easy to take but if you are riding long distances you will need to maintain your energy levels so you must ensure that you consume enough carbohydrate as well as your liquid intake.
- Hypertonic drinks are the slowest to empty from the stomach, typically with a high carbohydrate content (more than 10%). These drinks can provide plenty of energy but actually hinder hydration. They are best reserved for after-sport use when energy is needed but solid food is perhaps difficult to consume. Be careful of hypertonic solutions marketed as ideal fuel for ultra-distance athletes – they can reverse the normal process of osmosis in the stomach and can cause diarrhoea.

ENERGY GELS AND HYDRATION

Energy gels and bars are a popular way to keep carbohydrate levels topped up. But remember that the body uses water to store glycogen, so you must increase your water intake when taking these supplements. Check the packaging – if it states that they are isotonic then you should be fine, otherwise you could find that in your efforts to get energy on board you are actually damaging performance by dehydrating yourself.

HYPONATREMIA

You can drink too much. Your body can only absorb fluid at a certain rate, depending on whether it is an isotonic, hypertonic or hypotonic solution. Excessive water intake will dilute blood plasma and may result in hyponatremia (water intoxication) where blood sodium levels drop dangerously low. Taking electrolyte drinks and salty foods when riding will help to offset the likelihood of this occurring.

Sports drinks

There are many available commercial sports drinks and powders to make drinks. Try a few, as some may suit you and your needs far better than others. And be sure that you test them in training – competition or a long randonnée is not the ideal place to find that your fuel supply is causing you to dive behind a hedge every hour!

The ideal drink should:
- be palatable, something that you will not mind drinking
- not cause stomach upsets
- contain some carbohydrate (5–8g carbohydrate per 100ml) to keep your muscles fuelled
- contain sodium to replace salts lost in sweat
- be isotonic for most rapid absorption
- be cool (10–12°c)
- not be acidic or gassy.

Your body cannot process more than 70g of carbohydrate per hour (i.e. 35g in a 500ml bottle), so there's no point in making the solution any stronger. In hot weather you will probably find a weaker solution easier to digest.

Do it yourself

You can make up your own sports drinks:

- fruit squash diluted with 4 to 5 parts water with 1–1.5g salt (approx 1/5 teaspoon) per litre
- 60g glucose (or 100g glucose polymer powder, sometimes called maltodextrin) in 1l diluted sugar-free or low-calorie squash, plus 1–1.5g salt.
- pure fruit juice diluted 50:50 with water with 1–1.5g salt per litre.

For hypotonic solutions, halve the quantity of juice, squash or glucose in the above and increase the water content per litre.

Hydration tests

Weigh yourself before a ride and then again when you return – if you find that you have lost more than 2% of your body weight, you need to drink more when exercising.

Another simple test is to check the colour of your urine. A clear or pale yellow colour shows that you are adequately hydrated. If it is a darker yellow (and usually more smelly) then you are dehydrated.

Aches and pains

Health and well-being are vital ingredients for any sort of sporting performance whether it is a leisurely ride on a Sunday afternoon, a long-term expedition or a competitive event. On a long ride, small irritations, aches or pains can soon become major issues and can be enough to bring a ride to a premature halt. Deal with any issues before they can get inflamed and out of all proportion. You are far more susceptible to infections if your immune system is low, so be careful to avoid overtraining and recognise that many of these symptoms can indicate that you've been doing too much.

What follows is a brief A–Z of the 'usual suspects' that rear their heads to cause problems for cyclists – whether recreational or pro, most riders suffer from the same ailments.

Altitude

It is quite normal to experience a higher heart rate and breathing rate when cycling at higher altitudes until suitably acclimatised. Above about 1,800m (5,900ft) the thinner atmosphere makes it difficult to get enough oxygen into the lungs, leading to laboured breathing and lethargy. If you fly into a high altitude area, perhaps for a tour, cyclo-sportive event or stage race, allow yourself a couple of days to acclimatise before doing too much exercise. Fortunately, the body can adapt very quickly, and usually within 3 or 4 days most riders will be able to tackle almost anything without undue breathlessness.

Change in altitude is more significant than the absolute height gain. Changes of up to 1,500m (4,100ft) shouldn't present too many difficulties, but beyond about 2,500m (6,850ft) altitude headaches, nosebleeds, drowsiness, mental tiredness,

Cuts and grazes can be treated easily — it's usually advisable to stop to get patched up.

dizziness, nausea and insomnia can occur. Above 3,500m (9,600ft), reaction times and mental alertness can be 20% below normal.

It is easy to get dehydrated at altitude because your increased breathing rate accelerates fluid losses. The intensity of the sun is also greater at higher elevations so it is essential that you drink plenty and protect yourself with sunscreen.

Altitude sickness can be serious business, so it is always worth seeking medical advice if you continue to feel unwell. However, dropping in elevation by about 500m (310ft.) is usually enough to return things to normal.

Asthma

Asthma is a breathing difficulty (particularly breathing in) induced by pollens and other pollutants and may be triggered by exercise – which is not good for cyclists who are exercising in the open air. The condition can be controlled by prescription steroids and inhalers.

If you do suffer from exercise-induced asthma, take your inhaler and warm up progressively and thoroughly before making intense efforts. Let others know of your condition and what they can do to help should an attack occur.

To avoid dope control problems, competitive cyclists need to register as asthmatic with British Cycling or CTT. (Non-sufferers will not benefit from the steroids used by asthmatics!)

Back and neck

Back and neck pains are usually due to muscular strain or overuse, often combined with poor positioning, lack of flexibility, inappropriate technique or poor road surfaces. Sometimes these problems are due to degenerative wear or they may be non-cycling related, for example poor posture or muscle tension caused by stress, anxiety, depression or fatigue. Massage may help alleviate the problem but you need to find and eliminate the cause.

There are a few points that may help reduce the problem:
· do not increase your cycling distances too rapidly
· learn to relax on the bike
· avoid overstretching to the handlebars – raise your handlebars, use a shorter stem, move the position of your brake levers, and use different parts of the handlebars to provide a variety of positions to ease the strain on any one set of muscles during a ride
· remember your stretching exercises (see pages 74–77).

Although not conducive to performance, riding fatter tyres, lower tyre pressures or thicker padding on your gloves, handlebars or saddle can be used to counter poor road surfaces. If you have the money, carbon-fibre or titanium forks, frames (or frames with carbon-fibre rear stays) and seatposts may also help to take some of the sting out of rough roads. Some muscular pains may be due to trapped nerves, in which case you may need to consult with an osteopath or physiotherapist.

Broken bones

Without a doubt, the most common bones that cyclists break are their wrists and collar bones. It's a natural reaction. You lose balance and as you fall you put your arm out to break your fall. Which it does. By breaking – either at the wrist or the collarbone.

Riders will usually know when they've broken a bone, as it's often accompanied by great pain and swelling (although the pain can be confused with shoulder dislocation). Let the victim hold their arm in the most comfortable position and immobilise it with a bandage, or by rolling up the hem of their jersey to over the elbow, and get them to a hospital for treatment.

Cramp

Caused by dehydration, stress, overuse, injury, strain or staying in the same position for a long time. Cramp is a sharp, localised pain, most commonly felt by cyclists in the calf or thigh. If cramp is a common problem for you, check your diet and your position. Make sure you keep well-hydrated – tonic water (which contains quinine) or electrolyte drinks help many people and bananas (for their potassium content) are another useful weapon against cramp. Over-reaching on the bike or sitting too low can also cause problems.

It is possible to stretch out cramp once it strikes, but it is far better to avoid it by keeping your water and electrolyte levels topped up.

Cuts and grazes

Not unusual in any form of bike riding. Any fall is likely to result in some skin damage, particularly to knees, elbows and the lower leg. Most minor injuries will heal quite quickly. Clean wounds with water, removing any small bit of debris. Do not try to remove large objects but dress the wound and get medical help. If the wound has stopped bleeding, leave it open to heal in the air. Cover it with a sticking plaster if it's continuing to bleed or likely to get dirty. Apply a dressing and pressure with a bandage for more serious cuts, and raise the injured part above the heart to slow down the bleeding. Serious wounds will probably need medical attention. (See also *Gravel rash and road rash*, below.)

Drugs

Drug scandals have dogged cycling since Britain's Tommy Simpson died climbing Mt. Ventoux after taking amphetamines in the 1967 Tour de France. The scandal of the 1998 Tour, when the whole Festina team was banned for using Erythropoietin (EPO) and other drugs, has not helped either.

In fact, credit must be given to cycling's governing bodies for taking a more active and public stance against drug-taking than in almost any other sport or activity. After all, runners, swimmers, footballers and tennis-players have also been caught and punished for taking performance-enhancing drugs but rarely do their sports seem to follow-up and look in the dark places to flush out the suppliers or other culprits.

The simple way to deal with this issue is to stay well clear of drugs. But it is possible, as cases in the media have shown, that harmless-looking remedies and supplements can contain banned substances. So, if you are riding in competition, and use supplements or happen to be on any medication at the time it is worth making enquiries with the supplier, manufacturer, the sports governing body or the doping control unit of UK Sport to make sure that you are okay to race.

Eyes

Airborne hazards are common but avoidance is simple – wear protective glasses. There are many brands and styles on the market. You don't have to pay a king's ransom for a good pair, but look for glasses that are shaped to help deflect the wind past your eyes (rather than creating eddies of wind which will make your eyes water – especially if descending at speed). Some sports glasses can be obtained with prescription lenses for those who need them and many have interchangeable lenses for different light conditions, from clear for dark conditions, to amber or rose for low-light and smoked or mirrored lenses for bright sunshine (especially where the sun may reflect from light surfaces including snow and sand or when the sun is very low).

Wear glasses to protect your eyes, especially if you use contact lenses.

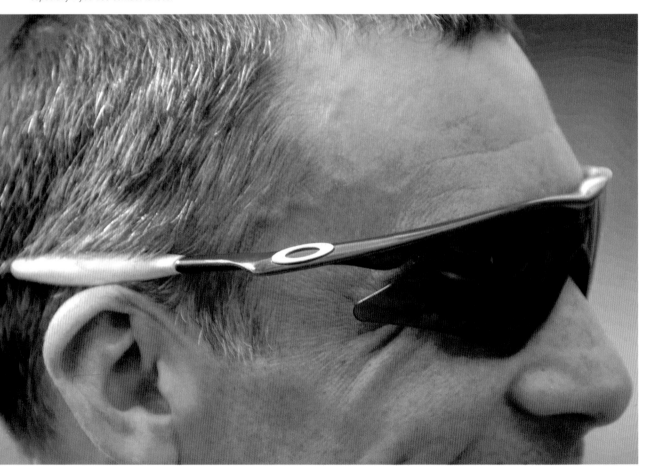

If you do get something in your eye, rub your other eye to produce some water to help flush it out or wash it with plain water or a specialist solution. If this doesn't work, lift your eyelid away from the eye and roll your eyeball around to help shift the item or you may be able to pick it out carefully with the corner of a clean cloth. Failing that, visit a doctor, hospital or optician.

Feet

Your feet are one of the three contact points with your bike so treat them with care. Correctly fitting shoes are essential: loose-fitting shoes can cause blisters, tight shoes will constrict your feet. Try on new shoes with your cycling socks – and go shopping in the afternoon when your feet will have expanded. Select your shoes by their fit and not by who rides the same brand or where the brand sits on the fashion-ladder.

Most cycling foot problems are due to restricted blood flow – shoes which are too narrow, wearing socks that are too thick or if shoe-fastenings or toe-straps are pulled too tight. Since cycling shoes have rigid soles for better power transfer to the pedals, precluding any running shoe-type cushioning, cyclists probably suffer more than most sportspeople with poor circulation in their feet. However the use of thin inner soles may help.

In winter, as there is no foot impact to stimulate blood circulation, the cold can easily penetrate the thin, ventilated uppers of cycling shoes. Prevent this by:
- wearing overshoes
- wearing two pairs of thin socks – if there is room in your shoes (buy shoes a size larger for winter socks)
- spray anti-perspirant onto your feet before putting socks on (this inhibits your feet from sweating and losing heat)
- rub warming embrocation onto your feet
- line your shoes with aluminium foil to reflect heat losses
- get off the bike and run up a hill to improve circulation
- use winter bootees with a high cut ankle.

Chilblains can erupt if you warm up too quickly, for example, by getting into a hot bath straight after a long, cold ride. The tiny blood vessels under the skin constrict in the cold, reducing the blood flow to these areas. If the skin then warms up too quickly, it becomes inflamed as blood leaks back into the skin tissues creating an immediate burning sensation followed by more prolonged itching, which is at best uncomfortable and at worst may lead to sores or ulcers forming. Avoid this by (ideally) not getting cold feet in the first place (see above), by taking a little more time to warm up again or by walking around a little to bring circulation back slowly.

In the summer the opposite can be unbearable – hot foot, caused by your feet swelling and their nerve endings being squashed inside the shoe. Avoid this by:
- using well-ventilated shoes
- remove the shoe insoles or cut a hole in the insole under the pressure point – the ball of the foot – to give your foot room to expand
- wear shoes a size larger than normal to let your feet expand
- loosen the fastenings – Velcro or ratchet fastenings can be adjusted on the move
- wear sweat-wicking socks.

On a long ride, you may want to remove your shoes from time to time to allow your feet to 'breathe'. But given the opportunity your feet will expand and may not return to your shoes so easily! If you require a foot massage on a long event do this one foot at a time and slip your massaged foot back into your shoe immediately after treatment before it has time to swell.

Occasionally, problems occur from poorly positioned cleats where this puts pressure onto the wrong part of the foot. Check that no bolts or fittings are proud of the sole where they could press into your foot.

Athlete's foot is a fungal infection. Although not life threatening it is unpleasant, causing itching and blisters between the toe and on the soles of the feet. It can easily be treated by powders and ointments but is best prevented by ensuring good hygiene practises at all times. Use only dry, clean towels and socks and wear sandals in places like changing rooms where the infection can easily be picked up on damp or wet floors.

Always wear gloves to protect your hands and wrists — in the event of a crash they will hit the floor first.

Gravel rash or road rash

This is a typical cycling injury, where a rider falls and loses a quantity of skin through sliding on the road, usually from the thigh or buttocks, which exposes the dermis layer of skin below the top epidermis. Like cuts and grazes, these injuries are usually more painful than harmful unless infected by dirt.

Clean the affected area and let it heal in the open air if you can. Take a painkiller for the first couple of days. Larger areas of damage may need medical attention. Keep your anti-tetanus injections up-to-date and protect the newly formed skin from the sun in the first year.

Hands and wrists

Your hands and wrists can suffer from aches and pains, tingling, numbness or weakness. This is usually caused by compression of the nerves in your hands. Many of the solutions suggested for back and neck pains (above) can be used to alleviate problems with the hands and wrists. In addition:

- avoid gripping the handlebars too tightly
- check your position is not too low or too far forward and that you are not placing undue weight strain on your wrists or holding them awkwardly
- padded gloves and cushioned handlebar tape or grips can help but don't have them too thick – you should be able to grip the handlebars so that you can touch the first knuckle on your first finger with your thumb without holding the bars too tightly
- where permitted, using aerobars can solve hand and wrist problems
- when riding, exercise your hands by moving them around, clenching and unclenching your fingers to improve the blood flow and relieve the pressure on the nerves.

Head

Whatever your level of fitness or skill as a bike rider, accidents can happen. Falling at speed, or even just awkwardly, and landing on your head can be serious. Your skull contains your brain and that is worth protecting. Always wear a helmet.

In any situation where a rider has lost consciousness, feels dizzy or suffers memory loss after a fall – however briefly – an immediate visit to the doctor or local hospital is vital. Avoid any strenuous exercise for 24 hours after the accident and ensure that the victim is not left alone in case further symptoms develop.

Knees

Knee problems are usually associated with overuse injuries, although they can be caused by catastrophic (external) trauma such as a fall or poor positioning on the bike. There are many possible causes of knee problems and even experts often find it difficult to ascertain a correct diagnosis. Riders who continue to suffer such problems should seek the advice of an experienced coach who should at least be able to tackle the problem by a process of elimination.

Helmets are compulsory for competition — and should be worn whenever you get on your bike.

Australian rider Boden Cooke battles on after sustaining a knee injury from a fall.

RICE

Rest, Ice, Compression and Elevation – should be your standard routine for many of the aches and knocks that you take on your bike. Follow this routine to help minimise pain and swelling and – with a bit of luck – reduce the amount of time that you will miss from training.

REST – take a few days off. You may not want to, but this is much better than further aggravating the injury which could result in being out for weeks.

ICE – use crushed ice or a bag of frozen peas, so that you can mould them round the injured area (place a cloth over the bag to avoid burning your skin with the cold. Apply this for 15 minutes an hour for the first few hours and then reduce it to 15 minutes every 2 hours.

COMPRESSION – use an elasticated bandage to compress the area, which will reduce blood flow and swelling.

ELEVATION – if possible, elevate the area above your head to further reduce blood flow and swelling.

Frequent causes of knee pain include:
- incorrect saddle height or position
- poor cleat adjustment
- using too big a gear
- using bent or damaged equipment e.g. pedals, cranks, frame
- anatomical anomalies e.g. different leg lengths, twisted spine or not using both legs equally.

An early complaint of clipless pedals was that the foot was secured too well and the lack of lateral movement caused knee injuries. Manufacturers responded with new cleats and pedals that provided a few degrees of sideways movement or 'float'. However, traditional toe-clips and shoe-plates never allowed any lateral foot movement either. The problem actually stems from the clipless systems not permitting any movement in a vertical plane and securing the feet very firmly on a horizontal (pedal) surface. In many cases problems were alleviated with the few degrees of float for the foot, sometimes compensating for poorly adjusted cleats.

DIAGNOSIS OF KNEE PAIN

LOCATION	POSSIBLE CAUSE	POSSIBLE SOLUTION
Anterior	Saddle too low	Raise saddle
	Saddle too far forward	Slide saddle back
Front of knee	Riding in hilly areas	Choose flatter routes
	Gears too high	Use lower gears
	Low cadence	Increase cadence
	Cranks too long	Use shorter cranks
Posterior	Saddle too high	Lower saddle
	Saddle too far back	Slide saddle forwards
Back of knee	Excessive float in pedals	Use pedals with less float
Medial	Toes point outwards	Adjust cleat to point toes in
	Excessive float in pedals	Use pedals with less float
Inside of knee	Clipless pedals too tight for easy exit	Adjust pedal tension
	Feet too wide apart	Adjust cleat position
		Use shorter bottom bracket axle
		Use narrower cranks
Lateral	Toes point inwards	Adjust cleat to point toes outwards
Outside of knee	Excessive float in pedals	Use pedals with float
		Use pedals with less float
	Feet too close together	Adjust cleat position
		Use longer bottom bracket axle
		Use wider (offset) cranks
		Fit 1-2mm spacer between pedal and crank

Penile numbness

This seems to be a big story in the popular press who make it headline news if ever the medical journals publish anything on the subject. In cycling circles, it doesn't seem to be such a big deal. Most cases seem to relate to extreme duration events (12- and 24-hour events and long-distance randonnées). It is a numbness and loss of sensation in the penis during, and immediately after, riding and may persist for varying lengths of time. It can be caused by a poor-fitting saddle or too much pressure on the perineum (the soft tissue behind the scrotum). Check your riding position – that your saddle is neither too high nor pointing upwards. Narrower, firmer saddles tend to provide better support to the ischial tuberosities ('seat bones') by reducing the weight resting on the soft tissue in front of them. Some riders have found benefit in using saddles with a central cut-out to avoid any pressure in this area.

Saddle sores

The most obvious area that cyclists (or non-cyclists) are worried about is the crotch and saddle soreness. Soreness happens through poor positioning, inappropriate equipment, overuse, or lack of hygiene. Choosing the correct saddle is partly a matter of trial and error relating to your anatomy, riding style and personal preferences. Comfort should always take priority over fashion. Avoid very soft saddles as these do not provide the necessary support for riding long distances. A firm (but not hard) saddle will be more comfortable and provide a more suitable pivotal point.

Prevention is better than cure for saddles sores — wash your kit after every ride.

By gradually increasing the frequency of rides and distances ridden your skin will become harder and less affected by the pressures of cycling. Surgical spirit (rubbing alcohol) can help toughen up the skin, but never apply it to broken skin. Wearing proper cycling shorts or short liners will help enormously. Experienced riders regularly use antiseptic creams (sold by pharmacists for bedsores or infants' nappy-rash) or 'chamois cream' from bike shops. Apply this directly onto your skin or rub it onto the padded insert of your shorts to reduce friction. Topical cortisone and products used to cure acne or fungal infections, such as athlete's foot, can also be highly effective in this area. 'Blister rings' can provide padding and relieve pressure off the sore. (If all else fails you may need to butcher your saddle by cutting a hole in it to avoid the sore point!) Saddles with a central 'cutaway' go some way to tackling this before it becomes a problem.

Infected hair follicles can grow into painful boils. They feel like a hard nodule and may have a pus-filled head. Soak the area in hot water to encourage circulation. If the boil forms a head or becomes soft it can be drained or lanced – this is best done by a medical practitioner.

Prevention is always better than cure, and hygiene at all times is absolutely paramount. The crotch is a sweaty area of the body, particularly when pressed against a bicycle saddle for hours on end and bacteria thrives in these warm, moist conditions. Wear clean shorts for every ride. Frequent use of antiseptic 'wet wipes' can be very beneficial on long rides. Change out of your cycling clothes, wash and dry yourself and your shorts thoroughly as soon as possible after a ride. 'Street clothes' should not be too tight either, but allow air to circulate. Consult your pharmacist or doctor if infections do not clear up within a week or two.

Paying attention to the causes of infection, pressure or friction and allowing time for the problem to heal will usually be sufficient to prevent further problems from arising.

Shop around for a saddle that supports you and is comfortable.

Stomach problems

Perhaps surprisingly, stomach problems account for more non-finishers of many long-distance events than any other cause. Sean Yates, the former continental professional and team-mate of Lance Armstrong, maintained that keeping well and having a strong constitution was an essential pre-requisite of any professional rider. A rider cannot perform if he's struck down with a stomach bug – and most problems can be avoided with some forethought.

·   Do not eat or drink anything in a race that you have not tried extensively during your training.
·   Allow yourself time to try out a variety of different foods.
·   Regular foodstuffs may not feel so good when ingested during the more intensive efforts of racing – have a variety of food available.

- Liquid foods are far more easily absorbed than solid foods but not all food mixtures are palatable or agree with everyone.
- Do some training rides exclusively using your race food. If you have a problem with a particular foodstuff try other alternatives on other rides.
- Prepare your stomach to the demands of eating in an unfamiliar position by eating when you train on your bike.
- Eat little and often. This is less demanding on the stomach than trying to ingest large amounts of food at infrequent intervals.
- Top up your energy reserves before they get too low to ensure that you are always adequately fuelled but never having to cope with too much food. (The same principle can be usefully employed in regular everyday eating habits too.)
- Use your water bottle. Drink frequently. Practise taking your bottle from its cage and replacing it smoothly and automatically so that you do not lose any momentum.
- Always thoroughly clean your water bottle, using a disinfectant or a sterilising solution. Do not share bottles or allow anyone to taste drinks from your bottles – the mouth is a hotbed of germs. Buy new bottles each season.

Sometimes you can't avoid a fall, but being prepared will help.

Index

flexibility   13, 72, 74
foot problems   171–2

g

gear ratios   51
gear selection   30, 32, 50
gearing   17, 36, 37–9
goal-setting   127–9
gravel rash/road rash   173
group riding   30, 31, 35, 39, 59–67
        changing over   61–3
        hand signals   65
        shouted instructions   64
gym work   137–8

h

hand/wrist problems   173
handlebars   11, 108
        height   11, 12, 14, 15, 16
handling skills   30, 33
head problems   173
health issues   167–77
heart rate monitors (HRMs)   130–1
helmets   18, 21, 113
hot foot   171
hydration   20, 108, 138, 164–7, 169
        at altitude   168
        when riding   67–8
hypertonic drinks   165
hyponatremia   165
hypotonic drinks   165

i

icy conditions   27, 45
interval training   40, 132–3, 136
isotonic drinks   165

k

Keirin   102
knee problems   173–4

l

lactic acid   73, 79, 80, 81
leisure rides   31, 155–6
life-style analysis   122–3

m

Madison   100–1
maintenance   16–17, 35, 37, 111
maximum heart rate (MHR)   130–1
micronutrients   163–4
motor pacing   40
mountain biking/bikes   14, 18, 22, 23
       cross country   6, 32, 53, 109–11
       downhill   6, 32, 112–13
       set up   11, 38, 51
       training programme   148–52
muscle fibres   35–6, 78–9, 80, 81, 83
muscle power   72, 73–4
muscular speed   72, 73
muscular system   78–9

n

90-minute race training programme   149
nutrition   20, 159–64
       calorie requirements   160–1
       timing   24, 87

o

off-road riding   21, 22, 36, 46–8, 58
on-road riding   21, 22, 42–5, 58
overload   86
over-training, rest and recovery   87

p

pace changes   30, 31
peaking   137
pedalling   35–7
pedals   12–13
penile numbness   175
periodisation   83–5
protein   160, 162
punctures   16, 20
pursuits   99, 101
pyramid training   135–6

r

rating perceived exertion (RPE)   85
rest and recovery   87
reversibility   87
RICE (rest, ice, compression, elevation)   174

road racing   5, 32, 36, 37, 90–7
        training programmes   139–45

s

saddle height   11, 12, 15, 16
saddle sores   175–6
safety issues   20–1, 92
        traffic   24–5
        weather conditions   25–7
self-assessment   121–7
        lifestyle analysis   122–3
        SWOT analysis   123–4
servicing   17
short-term muscular endurance   72, 74
six-hour enduro training programme   150
600km randonnée   157
skills matrix   29–30
slow-twitch muscle fibres   36, 78–9, 81, 83
SMARTER training   128
souplesse   36
speed wobble   55
sportive, see cyclo-sportive
sports drinks   165, 166–7
sprinting   30, 31, 56–8, 111, 136
        training programme   146–7
stomach problems   176–7
strength   72, 73
stretching   13, 68–9, 74–7
studio cycling classes   39
SWOT analysis   123–4

t

tactical awareness   30, 33
tactics   57–8, 95
tapering   137
10-mile time trialling training programme   142–3
time trials   5, 14–15, 32, 53, 58, 105–8
        set up   36, 38, 108
        training programmes   142–5
touring bikes   11, 36, 51
track riding   5, 21, 22–3, 32, 97–105
        fixed wheel bikes   38–9
        set up   16, 36
        sprinting tactics   57–8
        training programmes   146–8
traffic   24–5
training